Engaging Compassion Through Intent and Action

By Vanessa F. Hurst, MS

Illustrated by Merlin T. Lee

Wildefyr Press
Louisville, KY

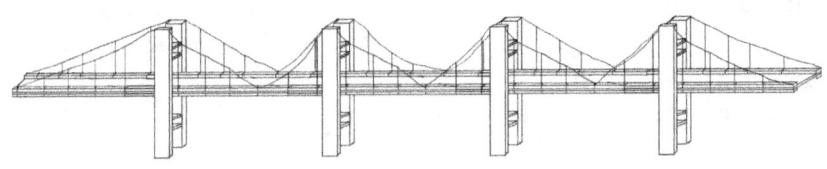

Wildefyr Press
Louisville, KY 40242

© 2014 Vanessa F. Hurst

Second Edition © 2016

Wildefyr Press is a trademark of Vanessa F. Hurst.
All rights reserved. No part of this book may be reproduced in any manner without the expresed written permission from the author.

Published in 2014
Printed in the USA

ISBN-10: 0990809102
ISBN-13: 978-0-9908091-0-4

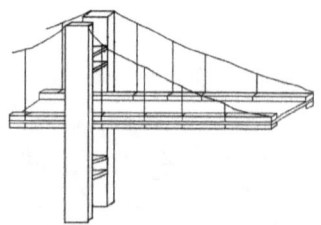

To my family, friends, and strangers who made the journey with me. Those who shared, stretched, or helped sync my vision of compassion include: my son Merlin, my fellow female orphans and male orphan, my beta readers, my editor Jeanne, G.G., the staff and customers at the Shelbyville Road Starbucks, and all the intimate strangers who are compassion's presence.

Table of Contents

Foreword — 1

Part 1 — 5
    Laying Compassion's Foundation

Introduction — 7

Chapter 1 — 11
    The Passionate Response

Chapter 2 — 23
    Compassion's Foundational Consciousness

Chapter 3 — 37
    The Transformational Power of the Life Pillars

Part 2 — 59
    Creating the Spans, Connecting the Pillars

Introduction — 61

Chapter 4 — 65
    The Gifts of the Spirit:
    Seven Compassionate Guides

Chapter 5 — 81
    Drawing Our Attention to the Present:
    Contemplative Practice

Chapter 6 — 99
    The Toolbox Found In Our Silence

Part 3 — 121
    Walking Across The Bridge

Introduction	123
Chapter 7 Transforming Our Personal Reality	127

Chapter 8
    Start Where You Are:
    Walking in Compassionate Connection
	141

Afterword	153
Biography	155
Resources	157

Foreword

My first memory of being fully aware and totally awake was when I was three or four. Kneeling during Catholic Mass, I chanted in Latin with the priest and the congregation. I connected to the Sacred, the priest, and the community of worship. Unconditional love and compassion surrounded me — at least until my sister jabbed me with her elbow! Although I was torn from the moment, the love and compassion of the experience lingered.

After a long journey of detours taken semi-aware of my reactions and responses to those people and events in my life, I woke up to the importance of being in the present moment. In that moment of clarity, I became fully aware of the world around me. This awareness of the present moment impelled me to no longer react from fears but to respond compassionately to the world around me.

When I was in my 20s, I discovered the power of a listening heart. Maybe I could not solve another's problems, but I could be present and listen. In those moments of awareness and intentional listening, compassion and love flowed freely from me to another and from another to me. During such moments of solidarity I felt a joy-filled connection with the other person.

While I would like to say I became a person of compassion immediately following that experience, my intentional listening and sharing of compassion were haphazard at best well past my third decade. In moments of mindful awareness, I listened and shared compassion. However, in my busyness I missed many opportunities to be a compassion filled companion. In rare moments of clarity within the busyness, I felt an uneasy turmoil.

Something was missing in my life. It was not until I was in my 40s that I had another epiphany — I became fully awake and aware to the power and importance of being present when reaching out to another. I began to remember those times, like when I was three chanting with the priest, that I intuitively understood the power of being present to another.

With this inner knowing my whole life shifted. My desire to be a healing presence became clear. I became committed to being more hit than miss in my awareness and sharing of compassion. To ground my awareness in the present moment, I began to use techniques from Christian, Buddhist, and pagan traditions. These practices helped me to create an inner peace through which I could mindfully share compassion with others.

In 1993, I made a life-changing decision by accepting a position at a retreat center operated by a community of Benedictine women. Over the course of the next fourteen years, the sisters gifted me with formal Christian contemplative prayer and the intuitive arts. I seamlessly integrated these new practices into my contemplative life. The writings of Thomas Merton also became an important part of my journey when I moved to Kentucky in 2007. Studying the writings of the grandfather of modern contemplative living expanded my understanding of being both contemplative and compassionate – they became two aspects of the same way of living.

When Louisville, Kentucky adopted a resolution in 2011 to join the Compassion Cities movement, I joined the effort to promote and praise compassion. As a member of Compassionate Louisville's Coordinating Circle, I have worked with a community of women and men committed to transforming others' lives through compassion. So for me, compassion is both a dynamic, living spirit and a lived experience.

How is compassion a lived experience? I best answer this question through my understanding of the connection between contemplative practice and compassion. Contemplative practice creates the silence in which compassionate action is birthed. Compassionate action sustains the environment in which contemplative practice flourishes. The image that best represents this connection

Foreword

for me is a bridge. As I journey across this bridge living in a transformative way, my contemplative intent and my compassionate action are aligned. I engage in compassion.

Within this book, Engaging Compassion through Intent and Action, is my blueprint for building a bridge that connects intent with compassionate action. I am not suggesting that you build the same bridge. I very much hope you will build your own. In the following pages I share what I consider key to living a compassionate, contemplative life. I have drawn upon ideas and practices from many others. I hope you will choose what resonates with you and design your own blueprint for engaging compassion through intent and action.

Vanessa F. Hurst

Part 1

Laying Compassion's Foundation

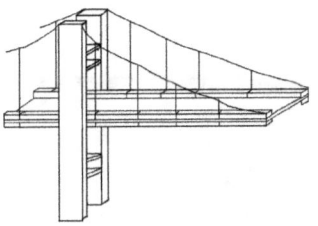

Introduction

Our compassionate heart is nurtured by our intent and our action. Both are equally important to our compassionate spirit. Of course, life interferes; we get busy. The connection between our intent and action becomes blurred. In life's whirlwind, we miss or ignore opportunities to share compassion. While our heart may be willing, our actions do not mirror our compassionate intent. What can we do?

Through conscious awareness, we lay a foundation on which the connection between our intent and action strengthens. We start by practicing awareness and letting our compassionate heart expand into the world. We envision a bridge between our intent and action. The image of a bridge is sometimes used as a metaphor for the spiritual life. Bridges are built across great spans; we may not even be able to see one side from the other. We trust that the bridge we cross is secure although we seldom think about the bridge's structure. Of course, each of its parts serves a specific purpose and contributes to the safety and integrity of the bridge. The bridge's substructure includes a foundation and pilings or pillars. On that sturdy base, a deck is laid and cables are strung. All of the bridge's parts, when built with integrity, ensure a safe journey.

Similarly, our compassionate nature is strengthened within the foundation of consciousness where we form our intentions. By adopting a foundational consciousness built upon certain principles, our life begins to reflect our authentic being. These principles are to cause no harm, to alleviate suffering, and to take life as it is. The foundational consciousness we create is a sturdy base resting upon several pillars. As we nurture our consciousness, the pillars grow deep roots into this awareness. Our conscious intent triggers action through the pillars.

Through ever deepening awareness, we engage our role as a sharer of compassion with our self, our families, co-workers, and members of our local, national, and global communities. This foundational consciousness, supported by the life pillars, forms the base of our bridge of compassion. As we cross the bridge, we live intentionally and begin to transform not only our self but also the world around us.

Foundational consciousness can be built with three simple agreements. We agree to cause no harm, to alleviate suffering in our self and the world, and to accept life as it is. When we agree to cause no harm, we are mindful how our words and actions are harmful or hurtful. We also examine our thoughts to see how they create both spoken and unspoken harm. The second agreement goes further. Choosing to alleviate suffering is the definition of compassion. As with causing no harm, alleviating suffering begins within us. Compassion, like love, begins in the home of our being. If we cannot be compassionate toward our self, how can we hope to lessen others' sufferings? Finally, we agree to accept life as it is. We are aware of what we can change and what we cannot. We acknowledge that we learn from the many life challenges and lessons only when we accept life as it is. We share compassion by embracing these agreements consciously and allowing them to change our personal reality.

This intentional way of living by causing no harm, alleviating suffering, and taking life as it is forms the base on which the four supporting pillars are placed. These pillars: being present, understanding who we are, living with curious daring, and taking a look at life are both guides and processes by which we fill our life with compassionate intent and action.

Life only exists in the present moment. We miss opportunities to live fully when we are absorbed by past regrets or focused on future worries. In the present moment, we interact with others and gain information to better understand our self. Only in this present moment, do we engage in relationships with our self, the

Sacred, others, and all of creation. These relationships provide clues through which we learn about our self and understand who we are.

We will not be open to understanding our true self without curious daring. Life is to be lived, and we only have the present moment. As we flow into the next moment, this one slips through our grasp. With curious daring, we live with gusto as we experience each moment with full and eager anticipation. Awareness turns our attention to the moment, and with curious daring, we are able to take a long loving look at our life, our reality. This look is not just cursory; it always takes courage to make changes that shift our reality. As we banish the illusions that we discover, we become a truer depiction of who we understand our self to be.

Being Present — Understanding Who We Are — Living with Curious Daring — Taking A Long Loving Look: These four pillars invite us into conscious, vibrant living. They are interrelated; and only together do they provide true support for our life of compassion. We engage in awareness when we live with curious daring in the present moment. As we take a long loving look at our self, we understand who we are and the many roles that we embrace in our life. As we bring our foundational consciousness and awareness to our work with the pillars, we live our wonder-filled life and deepen our awareness of the awe that exists in our self, the Sacred, others, and all of creation.

Any bridge must have a sturdy foundation to withstand buffeting wind and rain, rushing water, temperature highs and lows — the external stressors of life. Just like our bridge, our compassionate being is best created with a sturdy foundational consciousness based on the three agreements and supported by the four pillars.

Chapter 1

The Passionate Response

Passion is a loaded word for many. It can imply either sensual desire or irrational behavior. Consider how the word resonates within you. Does it conjure any images or specific feelings for you? Can you think of the word positively or as a means to describe your response to life?

When we live with passionate response, we are asked to willingly and radically use the energy of our passions. Living in passionate response means engaging our intense feelings for transformation. We are fully alive, fully awake, and hyperaware. Being passionate opens us wide to what life brings. With eager anticipation, we look forward to life's joys and challenges. We live with curious daring, eager to meet those joys and challenges in each moment.

Life is filled with challenges, disappointments, and uncertainty. With each life challenge, we are offered the opportunity to react or to respond. A reaction is without thought and is often hurtful and harmful to our self or others. A response, on the other hand, is filled with passion and conscious intent — that is, love. Such a passionate response is generated when we are at rest in our quiet mind. Within our quiet mind, we are aware of our internal monologue, the conversation within. Our quiet mind is a kind of incubator; within it rests our peace and calm and the means to defuse our reactions and to birth passionate responses. It is the home of our eager anticipation, curious daring, and wide openness. Within the quiet mind, passionate response emanates.

Responding vs. Reacting

Our willingness to embrace life with curious daring and to courageously commit to the great unknown prepares us to listen to our internal monologue. Our internal monologue is the ongoing, internal conversation that we have with our self. As we listen to our monologue, we become aware of our judgments, assumptions, and beliefs. By regularly listening to our internal monologue, our true self and our illusions are revealed.

As we listen to our inner monologue, we increasingly become aware of who we are. Our intuition engages in this safe place, and we become able to acknowledge our judgments and assumptions. As we become aware of certain scripts or repeating patterns in our monologue, we may choose to question some of our judgments and assumptions.

When others challenge them, we find that we have a choice: we can either react defensively or respond creatively. We need not react if we are challenged from without or within; we can respond instead. With this realization, our life shifts out of a box of our own making and becomes a limitless place of passionate response. As we consciously filter our judgments and assumptions within our quiet mind, we are empowered and choose to respond instead of react.

The more we engage this process, the more aware we are of the joys, happiness, and rightness of our life. When we holistically experience joy and happiness, our emotional, mental, and spiritual energies shift. We embrace this shift with a passionate intensity and are filled with an expansive lightness of being. As our awareness of the possibilities inherent in this path grows, we may commit to this journey of growing in passionate response. A feedback loop is created: our passionate response fuels our choices, and our choices fuel our passionate response. This cycle triggers the personal transformation that will positively affect others as well. We have engaged compassion through our intent.

Intent to Action:
Practicing Listening to Our Internal Monologue

Often I would catch myself wondering where some word or behavior came from. I might say or do something that I did not think was representative of who I am. For example, one night as I watched the news, I listened to myself verbally attack a reporter. In that moment, I also heard my thoughts behind my outburst. I intuitively used this awareness to my advantage. I began to understand my biases, my assumptions, and judgments. After that, each night when I listened to the news, I also listened to my internal monologue and reframed how I viewed the world.

That is how I began my practice of bi-listening: listening to the external conversation and my internal monologue at the same time. From then on, whenever I watched the news, I was aware of the judgments, assumptions and beliefs I held that might be triggering my reaction. With this practice, I trained myself to respond authentically, with greater understanding of who I am.

I engaged this practice at home and by myself at first. Over time, the conscious awareness of my internal thoughts began to seep into my daily interactions and conversations. Now my intent is to listen to the internal monologue and external dialogue in tandem.

Let us consider how such a transformation works. Through self-awareness and intentionally experiencing the feelings generating our passionate response, we access the power at the root of our passionate response. We are aware of how our feelings and emotions encourage our ability to respond. Over time, we notice how our thoughts, emotions, and even our physical bodies shift. We feel different. We create deep, abiding memories that enable us to recreate the feelings that stir the next passionate response. The positive experiences of passionately responding deeply imprint themselves on our mind, spirit, heart, and body. Because such experiences make us feel whole and joyful, we are eager to repeat them.

We make additional memories and, over time, we create and sustain patterns of passionate response. That is how we secure

the base of our bridge. Our passionate nature now flows from intent to action confidently. Our new pattern of consciousness is a cycle by which our memories nourish our passionate nature and our passionate nature nourishes our potential to create similar memories. Through each passionate response, our authentic being is strengthened. We are more quickly aware of when we
do not respond passionately. When we notice that our actions, words, and thoughts may have had a negative effect on our self or others, we return to our quiet mind for insight.

Our Quiet Mind

Actions matter. Words matter. But, thoughts matter most of all.

The roots of each word we utter and every action we take reside in our thoughts. Our thoughts are based upon our beliefs, our judgments, and our assumptions. When our mind is quiet, we become aware of our thoughts through our internal monologue. When we do not listen to what we are telling our self, we live from our subconscious judgments and assumptions. This may or may not be true. We may believe in something that is not real and does not reflect our authentic self. We may continue to react out of an illusion we have created — one we may have felt we needed in the past. However, only when we practice conscious awareness do we notice how a particular illusion is preventing our passionate response. Passionate response flows only when we are authentic and have a firm grasp on what is real.

If we are unaware that certain of our judgments and assumptions are false or inauthentic, it will be very difficult not to react violently or defensively when we feel challenged. We may even believe that our instinctive reaction is a valid response. Our ability to respond compassionately is limited when we are mired in illusion. Illusions imprison our authentic self; self-awareness is the key to breaking free and responding passionately in ways that are mutually life-giving

.

The Passionate Response

When we live passionately, we not only question with daring curiosity our assumptions and judgments, but we also courageously seek out and accept the possibility of living according to new beliefs. We live with wide openness and with a willingness to create a new reality in which our current way may not be the best way. We discover a new way of being by taking an intentional loving look at the real. We live a life of passionate response fueled by these discoveries.

Our quiet mind encourages us to question the authenticity of our beliefs, assumptions, and judgments. It does not matter if we have lived within the same illusions for minutes, hours, days, years, or decades. Part of our passionate response is to examine and reflect upon our assumptions and release what is not true. The understanding that grows from living the four pillars helps us to do this.

A friend once shared the story of growing up with his grandparents in the South. His grandfather was a member of the Ku Klux Klan. Needless to say, my friend's early years were filled with his grandfather's hate, prejudice, and racism. If my friend had continued to live his life based upon the judgments and assumptions he learned from his grandfather, he could have become a great bigot.

Yet, my friend chose to go to seminary where those beliefs, assumptions, and judgments were challenged. Through his education at seminary and with the help of new friends, he broadened his knowledge base and began to recognize and question his reality. With his stance of wide openness, daring curiosity, and courage, he recognized that his passion for peace and justice was not in alignment with what he had been taught. He named the illusions that formed his personal reality. His passionate response was to banish the judgments and assumptions on which his past illusions were based. He re-patterned his responses began living a more authentic reality.

A minister and professor, he went on to demonstrate during the Civil Rights Movement and taught at several seminaries. As an Old Testament scholar, he has written numerous books on interfaith relations. Because he passionately and courageously identified and banished his illusions, he became a model of peace and justice for many.

If I were to ask him what fueled his life-changing passionate response, perhaps he would say it was a strong desire for peace and interfaith understanding. What fuels a passionate response to life is different for each one of us, but at the core of any response is our desire to live life fully and unbound by illusion.

Our own passionate response is revealed as we examine our authentic being and realize how our illusions have impacted our view of the world. What form will our own passionate response to life take? The answers to this question can only be found through reflection and introspection in the present moment. The answer might change as we become more authentic, or it may remain a constant truth we were following all along. Discovering what is most authentic for us propels our passionate response to life.

Our Internal Monologue

How do we know what is authentic? Listening to the internal monologue within our quiet mind grows our self-awareness. Self-awareness in the present moment allows us to passionately respond instead of fearfully react. While it may seem easier to react without thinking, habitually reactions that are based on old patterns only serve to deepen our illusions and ultimately hurt us. We can break the chains of our illusions simply by periodically questioning our assumptions and judgments. This openness to inquiry slows our tendency to react in harsh, judgmental ways, and allows us time to formulate a passionate response. Gathering additional information by reflecting on our own experience as well as others' is vital to strengthening our authentic being. Responding passionately is not just a destination — a one-stop interaction with someone that goes well; it is integral to our lifelong journey to being compassionate. We walk this path moment by moment each time we choose to passionately respond to our self and others.

Sometimes the assumptions and judgments that are most illusory — damaging to others and to our authentic self — only become clear when we identify the unconscious fears at the root of our reactions. When we do react in hurtful words or behavior, we can take a moment to quiet our mind. We disengage in the moment and consider how to respond instead. It is never too late to shift from reacting to responding. We just have to remember our three agreements and the four pillars to engage our authentic self. We catch our reaction, shift to response, make amends, and learn from the experience.

We learn from both our reactions and our responses. Both provide opportunities for growth. When we take advantage of the learning gained from these experiences, living passionately empowers our ongoing transformation to authentic living. We live optimistically; we see each moment as an opportunity to be more true to our authentic, compassionate self.

Passionate living is a full-flavored, whole-body experience. As we engage our life with curious daring, there is no room for apathy. Engaged, eager awareness fills our being. We are hyperaware as we mindfully experience all the incoming sensations. We shift our perception and see our actions with new eyes; but, in truth, passionate living involves all five senses — and more.

Intent to Action:
Shifting from Reaction to Response

During his junior year of high school, my son chose a heavy load of classes. By early November, he often came home frustrated and anxious. It took me a while to recognize how my actions were fueling his feelings of discontent. I determined that however I might understand the situation, I could only alleviate his suffering by gently listening to him.

Some days, prior to his arrival home, I would sit silently to engage my quiet mind. I reminded myself to be a listening presence and to listen with the ear of my heart not my head. I also reminded myself not to judge him or the situation, but to just be present with him in his angst.

When I prepared ahead of time for our conversations, I noticed that my presence calmed him much more quickly. Following my cue, he seemed more comfortable and would sit in silence with me. That calm would dissipate quickly though, if I disengaged from the present moment. Then it seemed we would both trigger a reaction in each other, which we could only stop by taking a "time out."

We are well aware of the five senses that give us information about our self and the world: sight, hearing, taste, smell, and touch. Sensory input, including thoughts and feelings, may trigger either reactions or responses. Unless we are in the present moment, we may not be aware of how sensory stimuli affects us. We may be unable to identify the source of a noise or a smell, for example, but on some level the sensation distracts us. In these times, sensory overload is a real concern. When we focus our attention in the moment, we are more attuned to what is triggering our senses and are better able to identify and minimize distractions. When we are conscious of what our body is sensing, we are more inclined to respond rather than to react. Through our responses, we act compassionately.

Through this hyperawareness of what we are sensing, we begin to recognize our physical, mental, and emotional triggers and learn to respond rather than react to them. We can mitigate the distractions and discomforts that intrude on our quiet mind and choose life-enhancing responses.

What about our sixth sense? When we engage our sixth sense, we are hyperaware of the stimulus we are receiving from our five primary senses. Our response to this sense collective is less easy to identify than our responses to the individual five senses, but is every bit as important. Often our "sixth sense" awareness manifests as a knowing, a gut feeling, or an insight that has no factual basis. We may trust that this new awareness has surfaced to guide us, or we may have doubts. In either case, we can rest within the silence of our quiet mind and attempt to validate what the inner knowing seems to tell us. Trusting and validating are both important ways to cultivate our intuition and serve as guides for our passionate response.

We access our intuition with our quiet mind. Our quiet mind is a grand receptacle of knowledge — both what we have learned and what we can imagine experiencing. When we rest within it, we receive insights and are nudged to live more consciously and to respond passionately. The quiet mind directs our passionate nature in ways that accentuate our authenticity and shed light on our illusions. Without our quiet mind, our passionate responses cannot be authentic ones.

Living without the deep awareness present in the quiet mind encourages fear-fueled reactions that detract us from our life purpose. Living fearfully increases the discord or disharmony in our lives, while living authentically encourages passionate response and balanced living. When we engage each of our senses, including our intuition, consciously we are more able to make passionate responses.

Passionate responses bubble up from deep within the well of our authentic self. These responses come from an inner knowing and serve as a guide to navigate the challenges and overcome the obstacles we have built upon our false assumptions and judgments. Responding passionately is an intuitive act that requires us to engage our quiet mind with all of our senses. When we choose to ignore our quiet mind, we may become mired in illusion, and our passion may turn against us. Passion fueled by fear, worry, or angst may cause violent reactions and real harm.

Our reaction is usually not the result of our need to hurt someone; our reaction comes from the uncertainty and discomfort of our self-illusions. When we are overwhelmed by fear, angst, or arrogance, our fear-filled reactions that began as defensiveness may prompt aggressiveness. Emotions, although intense, have a short life. Ninety seconds is the amount of time it takes an emotion to move from inception to peak to release. We sustain emotions far longer by feeding them by our reactions.

When something sorrowful, angst producing, or anger-filled occurs, we can get stuck in the cycle of the emotion indefinitely, or we can ride the ninety-second wave with passionate awareness. That is, either we fuel the emotion, or we discover what it triggers in us. If we ride the wave of emotion without reacting, it will dissipate relatively quickly. Each time we fail to react, it gets easier to release the emotion. At the end of the ninety-second wave, we find our authentic self waiting. Our authentic self helps us to reframe the angst, sorrow, or anger we were feeling in ways that reduce our hurt, engender our happiness, and create a truer personal reality.

Bit by bit, moment by moment, we commit to recognizing our egoistic reactions and responding compassionately. We spend less time and energy on justifying our reactions and more on releasing the fears and illusions that trigger them. Although this gradual shift takes time, it brings us to a place of happiness and joy moment by moment.

Happiness is an inside job. If we commit ourselves to shifting our thoughts from justifying our judgments to passionately responding, we embrace what really matters — our authentic, compassionate self. Each time we create happiness and joy for our self and others, we create a pattern, a memory of what it feels like to be joy-filled. Every time we reinforce this pattern, we engage compassion through our intent and action: we transform our self and the world.

RI^2: *Reflection, Introspection, & Integration*

RI^2 is a contemplative practice that connects our body, mind, spirit, and heart in order to respond compassionately to something in our life.

First, we reflect with our heart. We identify what we feel without making any judgment about those feelings. We observe what is happening in our life and relationships that might relate to what we are feeling.

Second, we introspect using our logical mind. Again, without judgment, we attempt to understand what is truly amiss. We actively search for patterns of reaction.

Third, we integrate our understanding in a way that shift our fear-filled reactions to compassionate responses. More often than not, we change our thinking or behavior because we see that we were thinking and acting out of preconceptions about our self or others, rather than knowledge and understanding. This process, practiced regularly, transforms us. We become more true to our self, and more compassionate of others.

Use the following questions to reflect, introspect, and integrate transformation into your own life. Enter into a reflective place, where you just notice the many potential answers that reside in your quiet mind. Then engage your introspection. How do these responses fit with the reality of who you are? Which ones are authentic, and which ones challenge your illusions? Next, integrate what you have learned by embracing what is real and true and letting go of the unreal and the untruthful. Let go of the illusion.

Sit quietly and recall a person with whom you have had a recent interaction.

- Did you respond or react?
- What triggers powered your response or your reaction?
- As you reflect upon the situation, listen to your internal monologue.
- What were you saying to yourself?
- What parts of your internal monologue were accurate and authentic, and which were filled with illusion?
- How can you shift or release the illusion to create and sustain a more passionate response to the other person?

Chapter 2

Compassion's Foundational Consciousness

We all want it — that perfect place of happiness. We may envision our self swirling and dancing in Nirvana — heaven here on earth — a place without strife or fear. This ultimate place of being happy is gained by embracing life's chaos and, through it, finding a place of peace. How do we engage this happiness? How do we encourage the ongoing proliferation of peace and calm in the center of our being? How do we live out of happiness so that it expands past our core into the whole of our life and then spills into the lives of others?

We can begin to find answers to these questions by learning about the three Buddhist vows that encourage compassion through intent and action — the "three agreements." Pema Chodron's writings shifted my understanding of the three Buddhist vows in a profound way; so by the time I began to explore how to live a life of engaged compassion, those "three agreements" were essential to my life journey. They struck me as foundational to any life lived in relationship or within community. Whatever our particular tradition or vocation, the three agreements invite us to live a compassionate life by connecting our intent and our actions.

Cause No Harm, Alleviate Suffering, and Accept Life as It Is. Although Buddhist tradition specifically names these as the mainstays of a life of compassion, Buddhism does not have the corner on compassionate living. Like most religious and secular traditions, Buddhism encourages compassionate living based a moral code, some version of the "Golden Rule. I use these vows as the basis for the moral code that creates the foundation of the bridge connecting my compassionate intent and action.

Cause No Harm

The first agreement is to do no harm. This requires turning our focus to what is occurring now. In the moment, we become aware of our thoughts, words, and actions. With clarity gained in each moment, we begin to understand the ramifications of our judgments. Our understanding empowers us to accept responsibility for both the positive and the harmful effects that our thoughts and actions may have on our self, others, and the world around us. We realize our thoughts are the power-packed precursors to our words and actions. Causing no harm begins by attending to our internal monologue and disarming harmful words and actions while they are still thoughts.

When we choose to live from the maxim Cause No Harm, we agree to focus our attention inward, on our thoughts. Through careful examination of our thoughts, we recognize when and how we are sowing seeds of violence. Causing no harm means recognizing the potential for harm when we allow hurtful thoughts to prompt even more hurtful speech or actions. Stopping harm to our self and others at its root, our thoughts, is the first step of compassion.

With the intent to cause no harm, we begin to take responsibility for our thoughts and feelings as well as our speech and actions. We do this by engaging our quiet mind and listening to our internal monologue; we notice agitating thoughts and reframe our reactions to them into responses by remembering our intent to do no harm to our self or others.

Intent to Action: Listening Instead of Reacting

I have a friend who was in a difficult living situation. When she talked to me about the situation, I would be bluntly honest and, in retrospect, not very helpful. Instead of helping her move past the hurts she felt, my comments left her mired in her feelings of unworthiness and pain.

After one such conversation, I asked myself how I could provide support in ways that would uplift her. Using the RI^2 process, I developed a more compassionate way of responding to her that I integrated into our next conversation. Instead of offering suggestions, I patiently listened and asked questions for clarification. At times we just sat in silence. While my friend my not have found a resolution from that conversation, I believe she felt better able to respond to her living situation.

Awareness is the foundation of our quiet mind and what sustains our silence. Silence is not the absence of noise; rather, it is a place of deep calm, clarity, and the environment in which intense internal and external listening occurs. Within this deep calm, we foster our quiet mind — the place where we are aware and can respond from our authentic self. When we are engaged in peaceful silence, we are better able to recognize those assumptions and judgments that frame our inauthentic, illusory self. Once we recognize an illusion, we can reframe our reality and live more authentically.

The quiet mind listens on two levels — our internal reactions and responses and the external world. Our quiet mind enables us to locate, understand, and respond to subtler feelings and nuances we would otherwise miss especially when we are in the "survival mode" of reacting. Details and subtle impressions afford important clues to what we are experiencing and may guide our response when we listen to them.

For example, as a parent, I can become agitated in a conversation with my son if I focus on my perception of the issue. When I focus on his expressions and body language instead, I may discover what the root of the issue is for him. If my intent is to understand what he is feeling and address that, we usually shift to a place of peace. We connect through compassion. He finds resolution.

Of course, any of us can choose to survive in the world by simply making do with what we know and reacting when we are frustrated. Conversely, we can choose to live on a deeper level with openness and courage. The shift from surviving to thriving begins with our quiet mind. There we identify life's challenges and listen with our whole body to discover and implement creative solutions. Once our challenges are named and understood from our reality, we are able to construct loving, gentle responses. Our loving gentleness is not only for others; we practice this loving kindness inwardly, with our self. When we love our self no matter what, we sow the seeds of causing no harm.

Causing no harm begins with a commitment to not harm our self. We move through the fog of our illusions and act from our authentic, courageous self. Only when we are authentic, do we honestly examine who we are and fearlessly respond from our place of truth. Our authentic spirit moves us from survival mode to thriving mode.

Setting our intention to cause no harm may seem simple, but living from this stance can be difficult and even disconcerting. However, when we agree to cause no harm, we are charged with recognizing our hurtful behaviors, both subtle and overt. Causing no harm requires that we engage our quiet mind and grapple with life's challenges with honesty, courage, and humility. If we accept our self with humility, we are able to acknowledge mistakes. Courage then provides the impetus for us to rectify our mistakes and change patterns of thinking and acting that have prevented us from living as our authentic self. Causing no harm invites our authentic, courageous, humble self to shine through all we are and do.

When we identified a particular hurtful or harmful behavior, thought, or word, we name how, when, and with whom the behavior manifests. We engage the RI^2 process to better understand the harmful pattern and to shift our thoughts, words, and behaviors into compassionate response. The RI^2 process asks us to better understand our motivations and triggers — the habitual thoughts at the root of our behavior. Only when we understand those can we re-pattern our reactions into responses.

Unless we are consistently mindful, we may ignore or fail to notice our harmful thoughts and behaviors. We do not intend to hurt others; we are simply unaware. If we truly understood the harm that our words, thoughts, and actions sometimes cause, we would be overwhelmed by grief. Through an honest inventory and with diligent awareness, we temper our reaction and re-pattern the hurtful behavior into compassionate response. Through this effort, we lovingly respond to the world around us lovingly. We shift from a place of pain into a place of unconditional love.

All traditions teach the Golden Rule, which asks us to treat others as we want to be treated. We may collectively and individually believe in the Golden Rule, yet we all fall short. We intend to live by the Rule, but we fail to carefully examine our actions in its light. I regularly ask myself, "What part of that was compassionate?" when I reflect on my day. We need to examine our behavior daily to truly know how we are "doing unto others." Our accountability is transformative.

In our life we are presented with many opportunities for pain and for pleasure. When we are mindful, we notice our pain, the pain of others, and what we are doing to either minimize or add to the suffering. Regular examination of our words and actions invites us to acknowledge our role in our suffering and the suffering of others. We use this knowledge to alleviate suffering. As we minimize our role as a causer of harm, we position our self to alleviate suffering in active, productive ways.

When we vow to cause no harm, we accept that we are capable of hurting others, intentionally or unintentionally. When we commit ourselves to alleviate suffering, the second vow, we accept our wellspring of unconditional love. We can indeed help to heal others' wounds when we are also treating our own.

Our authentic self is strengthened when we acknowledge both potentials — to either cause harm or not and the potential to alleviate human suffering. When we commit ourselves to using our potential for great good, we become servants of compassion in our communities and in the world.

Alleviating Suffering

Being compassionate is simply, and not so simply, reaching out to others with the intent to lighten their load, share a smile, bring joy — to alleviate suffering. When we touch others by alleviating their suffering, we join them in solidarity. This solidarity is possible when we are in the moment and open to authentic sharing.

As we hurry from here to there, it is easy to lose focus on living compassionately. Life becomes about our schedule, our wants and perceived needs. We either ignore or are oblivious to the opportunities to alleviate suffering. The constant bombardment of stimuli pulls us into a place where reaching out and touching another in loving, compassionate ways becomes difficult. Opportunities to alleviate the hurt and suffering in another's life and to compassionately impact another's life are missed.

Being mindful and being aware in the moment, allows us to rest within our authentic self, the home of our sacred spark. The divine spark, the spirit within us, is an ember that connects us to all of creation. It is both the source of our compassionate nature and the energy that fuels our compassionate action. This spark connects us to the Sacred, and through this connection, to the person we truly are. When we are courageously authentic, the ember becomes brighter and fuels our compassionate intent. When our intent is brightly alive, so is our compassionate action.

Through awareness of the present moment, we wake to the understanding that we are beings of compassion whose natural response is compassionate. As we grow in this awareness, we consciously and intentionally seek out ways to be compassionate. These acts not only engage our compassionate nature but also grow out of it and renew the core of our compassion. The cycle of compassion is engaged. Compassion is both an outward movement and an inward movement: with it we alleviate the suffering of our self and alleviate the suffering of others. As we engage compassion through intent and action, our own store of compassion increases. Our compassionate nature deepens when we are a part of this cycle of engaging compassion.

For some of us, it is harder to receive compassion from others than to give it. As we listen to our thoughts, remember our words, and notice our actions, our compassion or lack of compassion toward our self may be revealed. We are called to seek to alleviate our own suffering too. This may be our most difficult compassionate act. Compassion is built upon self-love and acceptance. It strengthens our inner calm and empowers us to respond intuitively instead of reacting from our fears. We build and strengthen our compassionate foundation by sharing compassion with our self. Only after we love and accept our self, are we able to accept and integrate the love of others. Compassion begins with us.

I once attended a lecture given by Matthieu Ricard, a Tibetan Buddhist monk. One of the participants asked for guidance about sharing compassion with those who do not hold similar beliefs. He gently reminded us compassion is not a reward for good behavior. In other words, sharing compassion is not an intellectual activity during which we weigh the pros and cons of offering our compassion. We do not judge the suitability of another to receive compassion. Rather, compassion is the only just and viable response to any person's pain and suffering. We accept the responsibility and privilege to be a font of compassion no matter what the situation or what our assumptions or judgments are.

When we live with the agreement to cause no harm, the world of sharing compassion opens to us. With each compassionate action we share unconditional love. Our desire to be a compassionate presence grows. This strengthens our intent to be compassionate. No longer can we remain uninvolved with others: we enter into community. This community is comprised of family, friends, acquaintances, co-workers, and strangers.

Engaging compassion through intent and action requires a paradigm shift. We can no longer view the world as oppositional — us against them. We are asked to be aware of our judgments and assumptions, our angst and anxiety. In spite of our own doubts and concerns, we are asked to simply accept the world as it is. That very acceptance is the next step in deepening our compassionate stance.

Life As It Is

When I think about life as it is, I am reminded of a saying that has been attributed to the mystic Julian of Norwich, "All will be well and, in the manner of all things, all will be well." At times life is messy, chaotic, and filled with what we do not desire. We may attempt to hold tightly to our illusions and create a more palatable, if unrealistic, view of what life, our life, should be. That creation is a fantasy, which supposedly fulfills our desires and wants. Unfortunately it does not, because it is not real.

Chaos is inherent in life as it is. Of course, within chaos lies possibility. In our struggle to live life according to the illusion we hold to, we throw our life and authentic self out of balance. Until we accept life as it is, we lack the springboard on which to launch a life that is all it can be. All will be well when we align our personal experience of reality with life as it is. Only through this alignment will we discover the possibilities that are beautiful, right, and life-giving in our world.

Life is a wondrous roller-coaster ride that gives us both the greatest joy and the deepest despair, and every emotion in the between. We experience life's roller coaster only in the present moment. We can only enjoy this ride and move in alignment with our authentic self by accepting the joys and the sorrows and the in-betweens for what they are. This acceptance is the gate through which new possibility manifests.

Accepting life as it is requires us to integrate what I call the 4nons into all of our interactions: non- attachment, non-judgment, non-defensiveness, and non- violence. When we approach life with these four stances, our ability to respond is enhanced and our need to react lessened. Through the 4nons, we connect to our quiet mind and see our response flexibility increase.

Response flexibility refers to the pliability or ease with which we choose to respond instead of react. Between a trigger and our response or reaction is a pause. How we gear up to act in that moment is a result of our response flexibility. Our ability to respond is made brittle or inflexible when we live out of our preconceived judgments and assumptions. An inflexible response ultimately drives a hurtful or harmful reaction. If our fears and worries are triggered, our instinct is to react. We cause harm.

Each moment of cultivated awareness results in a more flexible response to life and its challenges. Non-attachment, non-defensiveness, non-judgment, and non-violence all increase response flexibility and help us to respond to life as it is, in loving, compassionate ways.

Intent to Action: Closing A Business

In late 2012, as executive director of The Merton Institute for Contemplative Living, I worked with a board of directors to dissolve the organization. Taking life as it is, I completed all of the necessary administrative tasks. When January 2013 dawned, life as it is became a very different reality for me, as I struggled to define who I was without the safety net of a job.

Over the following eighteen months, I had many opportunities to reflect on the experience. I also got involved in other activities I had not had time to enjoy before. I volunteered, continued to see colleagues, and made new friends. I gave rein to my creative spirit as well. This book would not have been written unless I had accepted my new life as it is. Has living the new life been easy? No, but it has focused me even more on living life with curious daring while engaging compassion actively and intentionally. Mostly, I have gotten to practice the 4nons.

The first non, being non-attached means that we do not cling to a particular belief, situation, or outcome. That does not mean we are detached or apathetic. No, we are simply wide open, adventuresome, and curious. We acknowledge our expectations with an air of anticipation. We are open to all the possibilities and gifts inherent in each. Non-attachment is a way of saying, "this is what I want, but show me a different, better way. I am open to living life with curious daring."

By embracing non-attachment, we are following the Chinese adage to hold life like water in the palm of our hand. If you have never held water in the palm of your hand, try it. Holding water requires a certain muscle balance and tension. The palm must be curved enough to create a bowl, and the hand's tension must be smooth and flexible. We realize that no matter how we hold our hand, the water eventually escapes. Non-attachment requires a similar, soft tension between our body, mind, spirit, and heart. We balance what we want with what life offers.

Non-attachment means we do not impose our wants, desires or expectations on life. Life is what it is, and non-attachment calls upon us to live within that reality. When we are curious and open, unknown and improbable possibilities float to the top of our awareness. Things that might have seemed improbable suddenly become possible. Being non-attached creates the potential for limitlessness possibility, great happiness, and unending compassion.

Likewise, non-judgment, the second non, does not mean ridding our self of our judgments and assumptions. Rather, we are asked to willingly suspend them. A stance of non-judgment prepares us to understand our triggers and the life patterns created by those triggers. We recognize that our judgments and assumptions are a result of our life experiences. Taking a non-judgmental stance allows us to peel away the layers of our experience to better understand how our responses and reactions mirror who we are. A non-judgmental attitude empowers us to see life not as happening to us but as unfolding with us. We are partners with life not servants of life.

When we look at life as unfolding, the more clearly we see the patterns we try to impose and the defenses we create to mitigate old hurts. When we choose to acknowledge our past hurts and to not react from them, we are better able to accept life as it is. We may still feel the pain, but we will not add to it.

The many ways our world is violent today are almost too painful to count. Violence can be as overt as murdering someone or as subtle as a snide, passive- aggressive remark. We will discuss non-violence more later. For now, we need to look at the times we are tempted to violence when life is, in our opinion, not as it should be.

A non-violent stance begins when we choose to be aware of our violent reactions no matter how benign we believe them to be. Once we are aware of the harm perpetrated by our thoughts, words, and actions, we can begin to discover and name the roots of violence within us. Such roots often lie in our disappointments, fears, and unmet desires. Only after we recognize what is at the root of our violent thoughts, words, and actions, can we rescript our responses to compassionately address our disappointments, angst, and fear. When we move from a stance of violence to non-violence, our worldview shifts and so does our response to the world.

When we take life is as it is, we struggle less and take advantage of more opportunities to create beauty amidst strife. Life becomes a chance to defuse potential violence and unveil the beauty hidden beneath the discord. We accept the challenge to practice peace and to serve as humble teacher.

When we choose to respond non-violently, we need to suspend judgment and to not assign blame. Even if we were the one responsible for an untenable situation, we choose to be non-defensive about our role. We simply accept responsibility for contributing to or causing strife. Accepting responsibility for the consequences of our actions requires courage. We accept our actions and do not attempt to justify or explain away our behavior. Being non-defensive enables us to learn from our behaviors and to change them. We cannot rewrite the past or manipulate the future. We can only live in the present moment when we accept life is as it is. We can only be compassionate in the present moment.

A non-defensive stance encourages others to contribute equally to a resolution. We practice non-attachment when we relinquish control and allow others to weigh in. We are mindful that our assumptions and judgments do not define us; we define them. Instead of reacting aggressively from our own judgments and assumptions, we remain open to myriad possibilities. We do not assume our way is the only way or our idea the best idea. We take the opportunity to be our compassionate best within life as it is. We cannot change life, but we can change our response to it and transform the way we experience it. Compassionate action does not erase the pain in the world, but it does alleviate suffering by reflecting the spark of unconditional love.

Again, living compassionately begins when we consciously and intentionally choose to cause no harm. We acknowledge the ways in which we are responsible for our suffering and the suffering of others. We choose to alleviate that suffering, through mindful action. We acknowledge that we may not always be able to be agents of transformation when we understand that life is as it is. Yet life becomes all that it can be for our self and others when we engage compassion through our intent and action.

RI^2: *Reflection, Introspection, & Integration*

RI^2 is a contemplative practice that connects our body, mind, spirit, and heart in order to respond compassionately to something in our life.

First, we reflect with our heart. We identify what we feel without making any judgment about those feelings. We observe what is happening in our life and relationships that might relate to what we are feeling.

Second, we introspect using our logical mind. Again, without judgment, we attempt to understand what is truly amiss. We actively search for patterns of reaction.

Third, we integrate our understanding in ways that shift our fear-filled reactions to compassionate responses. More often than not, we change our thinking or behavior because we see that we were thinking and acting out of preconceptions about our self or others, rather than knowledge and understanding. This process, practiced regularly, transforms us. We become more true to our self, and more compassionate of others.

Use the following questions to reflect, introspect, and integrate transformation into your own life. Enter into a reflective place, where you just notice the many potential answers that reside in your quiet mind. Then engage your introspection.

How do these responses fit with the reality of who you are? Which ones are authentic, and which ones challenge your illusions? Next, integrate what you have learned by embracing what is real and true and letting go of the unreal and the untruthful. Let go of the illusion.

- How did your response or reaction to the person or situation either cause harm or do good? Name the harm or the benefit that came from your action.
- How did you respond to both situations? Sit quietly and notice any body reactions. What is the condition of your emotions and your mind? How do your feel within your body, mind, spirit, and heart?
- What assumptions, judgments, and illusions prevented you from accepting life as it is?
- How can you shift or release the judgments, assumptions, and illusions in order to fully embrace life as it is?

Chapter 3

The Transformational Power of the Life Pillars

Each of us, over the course of our life, lays a foundation for our personal bridge. Each action, word, or thought either sustains the integrity of that foundation or causes minute cracks that weaken it. Across the moments and through the years and decades, we either bolster our life's foundation or, by our neglect, cause irreparable, even catastrophic damage.

How do we build and maintain a strong life bridge? We begin by laying a foundation. Our foundational consciousness is the concrete in which we will sink our bridge's supporting pilings, what I call the pillars. I have identified four that sustain and support a conscious effort to be compassionate: Being Present, Understanding Who You Are, Living with Curious Daring, and Taking a Loving Intentional Look at Your Life.

Over several decades, I unconsciously created a foundation, a way to maintain my intent to live compassionately. Before consciously identifying the four pillars, I unconsciously depended upon their support. Before The Merton Institute's closing, as executive director I had begun developing a program for contemplative living based on four similar pillars. When I began to write this book, I reflected upon those pillars. Using the RI^2 process, I discovered the four pillars that I had integrated into the foundation of my life bridge. As I used the RI^2 process as a means to living compassionately, I became more aware of the importance of the pillars in my life.

The fourth pillar, Taking a Loving Intentional Look at Your Life, is actually based upon a simple mantra of Jean-Baptiste de la Salle, "take a long loving look at the real." In truth, each of the pillars I use to support my foundational consciousness — *Being Present, Understanding Who You Are, Living with Curious Daring, and Taking a Loving, Intentional Look at Your Life* — I have discovered in the writings and oral traditions of spiritual masters, my conversations with others, and my own lived experience. For me, these four pillars that support compassionate intent and action are both personal and universal.

Being Present, Understanding Who You Are, Living with Daring Curiosity, and Taking a Loving, Intentional Look at Life are the guideposts that foster our intent to live compassionately. As such, they also support and encourage authenticity and self-transformation. Through being aware in the present moment, understanding the roots of our reactions and responses, meeting life with daring curiosity, and deepening or redirecting our patterns through a loving look at our life, we foster our authentic self. Only then can we engage compassion through our intent and action.

These pillars further support the three agreements we use to build our foundational consciousness – cause no harm, alleviate suffering, take life as it is. The agreements set our intent. The pillars ground our intent and guide our actions. In truth, the three agreements and the four pillars are deeply connected to and symbiotic to each other. All are integral to the foundation of our bridge.

When we are aware in the present moment of the four pillars, our life focus shifts. We become more open to what life is offering. We understand that a compassion-filled life is a lived life. When compassion fills every nook and cranny, there is little room and energy for regrets about the past or worries about the future. We respond in real time, hyperaware of the potential ramification of each choice. We build our life upon each present moment by expressing our intent through our actions.

By being mindful of the pillars, we are invited to passionately discover and to name our authentic being and then engage all of life with curious daring. We expose and release the illusions of our perceived needs, wants, and judgments. Curious daring opens us to the real possibilities our authentic life is presenting to us. We recognize our fears while examining our life's path honestly. Our patterns of authenticity and illusions are revealed through this loving intentional look at our life. With compassion for our self, we recall and recognize what we have learned and how we have either responded or reacted to life's triggers. By practicing the four pillars, we access self-compassion and begin the cycle of sharing and receiving compassion.

The pillars form our intent to engage compassion and live authentically. As our foundational consciousness becomes a lived experience, we are able to build the floor of our bridge's deck in the spaces between the pillars. The decks or spans we build form a personal reality that we continually check for illusions. These illusions are based upon judgments or assumptions that could weaken our life bridge. The awareness created by engaging the four pillars allows us to recognize what is true and what is illusory. When we find a crack, we fix it. We banish our self-illusion and rebuild a stronger deck. This lifelong process continues as we share unconditional love and compassion thus strengthening our connection between our intent and action.

While being mindful of the four pillars does not guarantee us an easy passage through life, we become more surefooted, more able to engage life with a passionate response, that is, with compassion. As we banish our illusions and lay a secure deck, the pillars help us to live in deeper, more profound ways. We no longer wonder who we are; we engage others and live in community.

We live contemplatively by living in conscious relationship. This way of being invites us to enter into compassionate relationships with our self, the Sacred, others, and all of creation. Through the pillars, we refine the skills necessary to be in ever-deepening relationships. We discover how intimacy manifests in our lives.

Intimacy exists on many levels and in many contexts. Often we speak of intimate relationships as those we have with our life partner, our family, or our close friends. The intimacy that evolves from living with curious daring is broader. It is any deep, heart and soul connection we experience with another. Such a connection may be a brief interaction with a stranger if the interaction is full of compassion. Of course, intimacy is also found in the long-term, deep connection we have with a loved one and with our inner self. Still, sharing compassion allows us many intimate moments of deep and surprising connection.

I remember one such moment. As I neared the entrance of Starbucks one morning, a gentleman waited by the door instead of entering. He opened the door for me. Our eyes met, and I thanked him. In that moment of our eyes meeting, I felt the love and joy of connection; I understood his heart and felt he understood mine. No longer were we two separate beings. We were part of something greater. Although I did not know his name and would never share a deep conversation with him — I might not even recognize him if I saw him again — we connected intimately, in wordless communion.

In that "Starbucks moment," I noticed how a stranger's welcoming kindness can have a profound effect. This touchstone moment reminded me that simply being present in the moment with another is an opportunity for transformation through compassion.

Pillar I: Being Present

Books have been written, seminars taught, meditations guided on the topic — being present in the moment. The practice has also been called being aware, engaging in mindfulness, or simply being here now. No matter what it is called, living in the present moment and responding with awareness is a most difficult undertaking. We are required to let go of the worries and regrets triggered by memories of the past and to not cling so tightly to our trepidation-filled thoughts of the future. We are asked to be aware of what is unfolding and to fashion a response not based upon past recriminations or future expectations, but to create a response filled with eager anticipation and daring curiosity. In the moment, we must recognize distractions while not allowing the distractions to pull us from the moment. All of this requires the practice of mindful awareness.

Most of us live with one foot firmly lodged in the past, mired in the mud of old worries and regrets, while the toes on the other foot are stretching tentatively toward the future. So, the weight of our life rests on the tips of our fear- illed toes! Then both of our arms and hands are stretched out to snatch our elusive dreams. Seldom do we recognize that we are out of balance when we expend our energy on past regrets and future concerns. Little energy is left for us to engage our awareness in the present moment. Because we are unaligned, we miss opportunities to use our daring curiosity to capture life's real possibilities.

Engaging Our Kua: The first pillar, Being Present, invites us to place both our feet in the present moment – literally and figuratively. With the correct posture, we can relax in balanced alignment. This alignment is what some know as the kua, the resting pose of Tai Chi. When we are in the kua stance, both feet are firmly placed on the ground, our knees are slightly bent, and our butt tucked in. Pressure is taken off the small of our back, and our weight is evenly distributed. We connect with our center of balance located just below our belly button and midway between our hips. As we practice the physical stance of the kua, we experience better alignment between our body, mind, heart, and spirit.

This posture physically supports our first pillar, Being Present. The kua posture, and the mind-body connection it empowers, fosters self-awareness and being present in the moment. It therefore helps us to share compassion. We are always poised to connect our intent with action.

Being Present. Choosing to remain balanced in the now, while acknowledging illusions that upset our balance, alleviates much of the stress in our lives. Practicing the kua reminds us of the balance we must maintain to be present. With this balance, our intent is compassion-focused and our resulting actions are compassionate.

Staying balanced in the present moment requires patience and practice. As our thoughts shift from the past or the future, we begin to focus only on the present. We may feel some strain, pain, or anxiety percolating within us. If we maintain our present focus and balance, what is bothering us may surface — whether it is a feeling related to a past situation or our hope for the future.

Only with practice can we remain poised in the here and now. When we are present, we discover more easily how to respond to our internal feelings in loving, gentle ways. Instead of wallowing in angst producing emotions, we are able to acknowledge and release them compassionately. Being mindful allows us to engage in practices that alleviate the angst, fears, and regrets swirling in our being. With practice, the kua becomes second nature, and we respond from this place of balance.

Aspects of our life may remain chaotic, but if we are in balance, chaos becomes a fertile place for growth; it cannot catch us in its tumult. While we cannot rewrite the past, we can resolve past issues and regrets in the present moment. We can maintain balance in the chaos of our emotion and confusion when we live in the moment. In the present moment we perceive what is truest about our self and watch our authentic life unfold.

Although being present in the moment one hundred percent of the time may be our ultimate goal; in reality, that may be an unrealistic goal. Even so, any time we choose to be mindful of the present moment, we reap real benefits — compassion-filled life patterns. When we are here now, we notice what wants to pull us out of balance. When we are here now, we have the presence of mind to make decisions that positively impact our life. Most of all, this first pillar focuses our awareness on the real, a goal of living contemplatively.

All contemplative practices serve to bring us to a place of peace-filled calm and silence. Through such practices we expand our quiet mind. An engaged, quiet mind focuses our attention on the present moment and nothing else. Contemplative practices vary. Some include sitting in silent meditation, others engaging in dialogue, or even running a marathon — anything that stimulates mindfulness. All contemplative practice invites us to connect to the silence within, the place of our quiet mind — the gateway to the present moment. In this place, we are capable of achieving hyper-awareness. With a heightened awareness, we notice what is unfolding in our life and are able to respond instead of react. Emotions of angst, fear, worry, and regret are released without harm to ourselves or others when we choose to respond instead of react.

By being in the moment, we are better able to identify what brings us to a place of calm and what triggers angst and fear within us. Our ability to respond instead of reacting increases when our quiet mind is engaged. We notice the chaos that comes from a state of busyness or feelings like angst and anger. An engaged quiet mind can respond to the chaos in a different way than one that is untutored and untrained. Engaging in one or more contemplative practices allows us to create a pathway for responding to the root causes of our fear and anxiety and relieve the pressure they put on us to react without compassion for ourselves or others.

Being present is an ongoing journey of listening to our thoughts and attending to our words and actions. However, mindfulness involves more than focusing on our own thoughts and actions. We become aware of how others are either responding or reacting as well. Our engaged awareness helps us to keep our balance even when others are not keeping theirs, and most importantly, to respond compassionately.

In summary, living in the present moment is the beginning of self-awareness. Through this pillar, we gather the information needed to understand who we are and how we have formed our judgments, assumptions, and motivations. This pillar enables us to recognize our illusory judgments, assumptions, and agendas. Through this self-awareness, we form our compassionate intent. One byproduct is a growing understanding of how to respond from our authentic self.

Pillar II: Understanding Who You Are

In one sense, our life is a huge canvas on which we paint layer upon layer of meaning. Each image created is the result of either reacting or responding to our self, others, and life as we experience it. Once we view and interpret one image's subtle nuances, our eyes light upon another portion of our life painting. We alter one image, and another changes. The portrait of our life is constantly being created and reworked. As we gain a greater understanding of who we are, our vibrant portrait becomes evermore true-to-life.

When we are unaware of who we are, it is as if certain images we paint are discolored or blurred. These are the illusory judgments and assumptions we hold that detract from our life's portrait. When we are authentic in the present, our perception of reality renders an accurate picture.

Of course illusions are real in one sense. They have real ramifications for our life. We may only recognize their illusory nature when we begin to paint an authentic picture of our life. The illusions simply do not fit; they do not improve the picture's composition; they do not add meaning or beauty to our life portrait. In time, we decide to paint over them.

Being in the moment . . . engaging in reflection and introspection leads us to understand who we are. Practicing this awareness can effect change on deep internal levels. In this place, we recognize our authentic being and distinguish our authentic self from our illusions. When we are in the moment, we are able to strip away our illusions and stand in our authentic truth. The process may be uncomfortable, but the end result is worthwhile.

Accepting who we are frees our authentic self by revealing the flaws we try to hide behind various illusions. Our flaws themselves are not negative; rather, they provide insight into our own humanness. We do not need to paint over our flaws — they make us who we are, and we learn from them. As we embrace an accurate image our own humanness, we become more authentically compassionate to our self and others.

The Transformational Power of the Life Pillars

I have developed a straightforward process for looking at what I need, either within myself or in my relationships with others, to be able to grow in compassion. The process of RI² — reflection, introspection and integration — is a way of revealing and understanding the authentic self that rests in the center of our being. With RI² we discover within our self places of balance and imbalance. In those places reside our responses and our reactions. We use this knowledge to grow in authenticity. The self-awareness gained by practicing RI² is the self compassion force behind our compassionate transformation.

Using the RI² Process: Reflection

Reflection invites us to hear with the ear of our heart, to engage in what I call full body listening. We listen with all of our senses and process any information we gather within our quiet mind. While we pay attention to the words that we and others utter, we are also aware of nonverbal aspects of our dialogue and any hidden nuances within the message.

Through the ear of our heart we listen realizing that what is most important is often unspoken. We reflect on what we hear and do not hear, and we are open to the deeper, unspoken meanings. We respond to others' words and actions compassionately, knowing that there is much we do not know.

The Sacred present in all things is revealed when we are not attached to any specific knowing. Reflection is the avenue through which we dare to find a way to respond to life in transformative ways. It requires non-attachment. We might reflect on what we want or do not want, but we allow life to show us what we truly need. We are open to the possibilities that may change us and increase our understanding of life in the present moment.

Non-attachment, the first of the 4nons, is essential to the practice of reflection. It requires us to let go of our arrogance and feelings of entitlement. We release the idea that our perceived reality is totally truthful and accurate. We realize that life is not only about us. No longer do we disregard what is happening in the periphery of our existence. We look at life, in the middle and within the margins, with impartiality and openness.

Reflection pushes us past our self-imposed limits and invites us to pay attention without judgment to what is revealed. In this place, we intentionally suspend our judgment as we gather information. We are not defensive about our beliefs. Our goal is simply question why we choose to react or respond in a certain way rather than intuitively or authentically. We respond intuitively by listening to our internal voice, that is, the nudges that are often nonverbal and flow from our divine spark — the center of our compassionate intent.

Entering and remaining in a place of reflection is possible when we attend to the breath. Awareness of our breathing allows us to notice any turmoil that is occurring in our life. Focusing on the breath is the gateway the reservoir of silence in our quiet mind. Within this space, our intuitive response dwells. The silent sacred whispers well up. We hear not only what is said but also what is meant. When we reflect within our quiet mind while non-attached, we may be astonished by what resides in our subconscious.

Engaging in reflection at set moments throughout the day empowers us to practice ongoing reflection in the present moment. If we choose three ten-minute reflection times — in the morning, at noon, and in the evening — we create anchor points of awareness. This regular practice helps us maintain awareness throughout the day. In time, as we train our minds to engage in reflection, our moments of awareness flow into the spaces between reflection times. Our actions reflect the strong connection between our intent and action. After a while, practicing reflection becomes second nature. Our compassionate intent infuses our life and fuels compassionate action.

Using the RI² Process: Introspection

The next step in the RI² process is introspection. While reflection is a way of deepening our awareness of how we respond and react, introspection helps us to better understand who we are and why we respond and react. Through introspection we begin to know our self — our uplifting, positive facets as well as our fears and flaws. The key to introspection is the cultivation of a non-defended, non-judgmental attitude. Introspection within the quiet mind activates our intuition, which help us to discern ways to live more authentically. Through introspection we take a compassionate look at our self; it is not an excuse to dwell on our faults and become mired in despair.

Introspection invites us to notice and own our judgments, assumptions, and behavior patterns without judging them. We acknowledge them, which is not the same as defending them. Through introspection we deepen our attitude of non-attachment. When we are non-attached, we can accurately review our judgments and assumptions while recognizing their validity or falseness. During this review or assessment, we do not defend our choices. Instead, we seek to understand why we made those choices. We decide whether we want to make different ones.

While practicing introspection, each of us begins exactly where we are in the present moment. Acknowledging where we are may be painful. We have spent a lifetime of creating and sustaining life patterns, many of which are not life giving. Perhaps at one time they helped us to survive. Now we have opportunities to make choices that are life giving — ones that help us to thrive. We have to identify which behaviors, patterns, and choices are detrimental to us before we can release them.

Not all inauthentic behaviors are cringe-producing; some are more difficult to identify. For example, we may be very helpful to everyone around us, but after helping become resentful. Being hyper-helpful may be an inauthentic behavior born out of our fear of not being needed.

Through this resource we understand life patterns and find new opportunities for transformation. Introspection helps us to understand our self, so we better evaluate what choices and behaviors are authentic for us. With that understanding, we are able able to recommit to what is beneficial to our life journey and avoid what may no longer work for us or is actually harmful.

With the first step, reflection, we engage our inquisitive mind and explore our world with curious daring, and without preconceptions. We do not judge our self or our behaviors. With the second step, introspection, we look at our choices and, again try to understand why we made them. Without judgment we ask, what did we believe or assume about our self? Is what we assumed true? If it was true then, is it now?

During introspection we notice the judgments and assumptions we are still caught in. We evaluate how those judgments and assumptions impact our life. We decide to change what is not working.

If we have spent any time on this planet interacting with others, reading, watching TV, engaging the world outside, we have formed judgments and made assumptions. We have constructed our own understanding of life and our place in it. This personal reality is comprised of both authentic and illusory parts.

Introspection invites us to identify what may be false and have negatively impacted our interactions with our self, others, the Sacred, and all of creation. With curious daring, we make a commitment to understand our self through introspection. With new understanding of our inner self, including our motivations, we can decide to integrate this understanding, which may change our life profoundly.

When we engage in introspection, we recognize which judgments are valid and which are preventing us from living authentically. The difficulty with judgments and assumptions is their potential to trigger suffering for our self and for others. Usually judgments and assumptions are not instruments of compassion. They serve as the basis for harmful and hurtful reactions. Introspection provides the means to logically assess our judgments and identify which are true and which are detrimental.

In hindsight, we might either laugh or be embarrassed by some of our past assumptions and judgments. Introspection invites us to appreciate how human we are. It stimulates self-compassion. We know we are not intentionally cruel, nor do we intentionally inflict suffering on others. We simply get caught up in our perceived reality and live life bouncing from one reaction to another. Hurtful behavior happens when we are living anywhere but in the moment. Through introspection we choose to live in the present, and find balance in the here and now. We stop bouncing around when our defenses are triggered; we stop overreacting.

Practice is everything. Continual reflection and introspection help us to gain a greater understanding of who we are and how we interact with the world. Constant and deeper reflection and introspection reveal more intimate, often unacknowledged facets of our self. The material gained from this process can be used to shift fearful reactions to intuitive responses. When we make these shifts in behavior, we engage in the final step, integration.

Using the RI² Process: Integration

Consciously and unconsciously we choose how we will respond to life's unexpected challenges. When we are aware, our responses are conscious. When we are focused on past regrets or future concerns, we react without self-awareness. Reflection and integration invite us to be present and to formulate responses out of awareness and understanding. We actively integrate the self-understanding we gain from reflection and introspection and re-pattern our thinking to better engage compassion through our authentic self.

Only through the integration of our knowing (reflection) and our understanding (introspection) can true, sustainable transformation occur. Through these two steps, we recognize our life triggers and better understand our reactions to them. Integration of the knowing and understanding strengthens our intent to be agents of compassion. We undergo a paradigm shift. Within this new paradigm, we gain tools to intuitively respond to life's challenges.

Integration is an ongoing opportunity to modify the harmful, destructive, hurtful patterns we identify. Now we commit to integrating the understanding we gain, by taking every opportunity to respond from our authentic center. We not only shift away from the false judgments and assumptions that drove us in the past, we begin to actively and purposefully choose to respond to our self, to others, to life in loving, gentle ways. If we are to integrate compassion fully, we must always work to reach a place of understanding with the other, whatever our differences. Integrating compassion more fully into our life takes curious daring.

Pillar III: Living with Curious Daring

Living with curious daring requires making a commitment to keeping our hearts and minds open. Within this place of wide openness, we meet each moment with a full-body smile and an eagerness to embrace the unknown. We engage our self and others in compassionate, caring, and uplifting ways. We incorporate our foundational awareness: causing no harm, alleviating suffering, and taking life as it is, when living with curious daring.

RI^2, the process of reflection, introspection, and integration, encourages a deep knowing of our self. When we reflect and introspect, hidden or avoided parts of our self are revealed. As we reflect and introspect, we begin to see how our thoughts, words, and actions impact us and the individuals and situations in both our personal sphere and in the greater world. Any shift we make in our thoughts, words, and actions has the potential to stimulate a radical shift in our sphere of influence. Curious daring impels us to make that shift.

Curious daring invites us to use the RI^2 process to reframe our life situations. We are challenged to birth possibilities by eschewing our negative misconceptions. We listen with an open heart to discover what and who engages our enthusiasm. This full body listening helps us form our intent to respond with openness. We respond to those cues that float on the whispers of the Sacred and lift us into the conscious stream of awareness; then, with curious daring, we act on them.

When we engage our curious daring, we enter the place of the beginner's mind — a place of childlike awareness coupled with enthusiasm for learning. With a beginner's mind, we are open and eager to experiment and to try new things. No longer risk adverse, we enter a place of limitless possibility and new beginnings, we engage our curious daring to transform our self and provide transformative nudges to others.

In our beginner's mind, we suspend our judgments and let go of our agendas. Our purpose is to live in joyful resonance with others and the world. We are not king/ queen of the hill. We become one with the hill, every blade of grass, rock, speck of dirt is one with us. We understand that we are not only an individual but also a vital, intentional part of the world community. As part of a community everything that we do impacts others in apparent and subtle ways. We are vitally connected to all.

Within this matrix of connection, we impact others through our compassionate actions. When we live with curious daring, we encourage others to enter into compassionate presence. The impact of our compassion increases. Our personal responses propelled by curious daring move our community in a new direction, set it on a new path. The curious daring that is grounded in our authentic spark invites others to rest in peaceful awareness and engage their curious daring, too. The dynamic synergy of curious daring transforms us both as individuals and as a community.

The third pillar, *Living with Curious Daring*, is important when we commit to integrating our new self understanding and changing any way of thinking or acting that is inauthentic. Without curious daring we may lack the courage to make such a change. Fortunately, the enthusiasm we tap into by becoming more aware of our authentic self is enough — more than enough — to move us forward. For it is exciting to engage curious daring, to have a new lease on life and be filled with compassion for our self. Now we come to the final pillar: Taking a Loving Intentional Look.

Pillar IV: Taking a Loving Intentional Look

This pillar is our self-check: How are we doing? We reflect, we introspect, we integrate what we learn. Finally, we take a realistic look at how we are doing. Are we living authentically with curious daring, or do we suspect there is something we are still not seeing — some illusion we have not named?

The fourth pillar reminds us to lovingly and gently engage the RI^2 process. It is a process we may reinitiate at any time, whenever we need to examine our life in order to live more authentically. Like the other three, this pillar is engaged through awareness in the present moment. Although we may look backward over our life to gain self-understanding, we remain focused on the present moment. We need to be aware of what we are feeling as we engage this process of recollection. Those feelings provide important clues. Taking a loving intentional look at our life is not always easy or comfortable. It, too, requires curious daring.

Indeed, the third pillar, Living With Curious Daring, is active when the fourth pillar is truly engaged. Curious daring opens our awareness on progressively deeper levels, so that we might see the impact our compassionate intent and action have had on the world.

Taking a loving intentional look is being aware of the world and our impact on it — not just its impact on us. We identify what is authentic and uncover persistent illusions. We recognize patterns we create and sustain by our reactions and responses. Taking an intentional look may allow us to neutralize the impact of our reactions and deepen the impact of our responses. Through this intentional look, we identify the patterns whether beneficial or harmful. After reflection and introspection, we integrate our understanding in ways that shift our behavior. At any location on our bridge, we can take a loving intentional look to ensure that we are living authentically.

Taking an Intentional Look: Recognizing

First, we recognize and name what is "right" in our life and identify what needs to shift. Next, we release whatever behavior or thought causes harm. We reaffirm behaviors and thoughts that are authentic and loving. Finally, we respond to life with renewed compassion.

It is difficult to be objective about one's own life. We have a myopic view. Some details are simply too close to us to see accurately. We may be tempted to change or embellish our life narrative to make it more palatable.

Taking a loving intentional look means consciously recognizing what our actions, words, and thoughts reveal about us. We gain a basic self-understanding of our life's patterns and the choices we continue to make. But, we may not yet understand what our choices mean or the purpose they serve. Some may be basic survival mechanisms. Others might encourage continuous growth while others create stagnation.

Through our intentional look, we identify the purpose of any life pattern. This first step — recognition — is accomplished without judgment. We continually try to identify those judgments and assumptions that tend to trigger a defensive reaction within us. We want to understand whether these defenses serve any life-affirming purpose. Only then can we decide what we want to change.

This stage requires us to reflect and introspect as we gain a greater understanding of who we are. Once we understand who we are, we are capable of making decisions that rescript the patterns and deepen our compassionate stance.

Recognizing our defensive patterns is not an excuse to dwell on past hurts or excuse our own reactive behavior. This step requires that we be non-attached and non-defensive. After we undertake a fact-finding mission, we engage our curious daring to identify what we need to release and what can be re-affirmed. Awareness in the present moment creates the environment in which we can accurately identify the behaviors that impact our life patterns.

Again, such patterns are not always harmful. Our patterns can be positive and transformative. Discerning the role our patterns play in our narrative requires honestly examining how our patterns influence us now.

Taking an Intentional Look: Releasing or Reaffirming

Once we recognize a behavior and the role it plays in creating a life pattern, we must decide if the pattern is life-giving or life-depleting. Only we can answer this question. Before answering, we must search for the roots of the pattern and identify the triggers that stimulate our negative reactions. However, taking an intentional look requires more than simply answering "yes" or "no" to the question. Is this pattern an authentic one? After answering this question, we must respond in one of two ways: we choose a strategy for releasing the actions, words, or thoughts that sustain a negative pattern or we find a way to reaffirm a beneficial pattern.

Our life scripts are not instantaneously rewritten. Patterns modified take time to integrate into our life path. Patterns are created over years, decades. In order to reroute the patterns, we must practice patient awareness over many moments. The old saying it is never too late to learn may be true, but change takes time.

Of course, not all patterns need to be drastically changed. Some only need minor adjustment. We always look at the totality of the pattern when discerning what pattern shifts need to occur. A pattern may have both positive and life-depleting aspects; we consider both prior to initiating a shift. Freeing our self from even one negative aspect of a harmful pattern injects hope into our life and promotes self-transformation. Releasing harmful behavior becomes easier with practice although letting go of old habits is never without pain. We may even feel grief.

Taking a loving intentional look also requires that we notice, name, and own the parts of our reality of which we are proud. We practice humility by noticing and naming the good that resides within us. We consciously name what is right in our life and affirm patterns that are life giving. We always affirm our self when we are authentic, courageous, and humble. Self-affirmation is vital when taking a loving intentional look at our life.

Taking an Intentional Look: Responding

By taking an intentional look, we become even more aware of our ability to choose. The more often we respond to life's challenges instead of reacting to them, our capacity for responding increases. Choosing to respond instead of react improves with practice. Our goal is to increase the frequency of our compassionate responses.

Responding results when we foster awareness within our quiet mind. We listen with all six senses and are able to distinguish what is true from what is false. Sometimes what we are reacting to is both satisfying and angst-producing. Be wary when reacting feels good or self-affirming because this feeling is likely based upon illusion. A defensive reaction is never beneficial. Of course, angst may build for some time before we actually react to what is bothering us. Through our intentional look, we become aware of what the trigger is, what we are attached to. With this awareness, we take steps to release the pressure in order to limit our reactions. We choose compassion instead.

When we incorporate the pillars into our daily life, we become aware of our triggers and their roles in our responses and our reactions. This is the goal of taking a loving intentional look — to notice what we tend to react to and choose to respond from our quiet mind in loving, gentle, compassionate ways. Through the process of RI^2 we strengthen our response flexibility and more fully engage compassion through our intent and action.

RI^2: Reflection, Introspection, & Integration

RI^2 is a contemplative practice that connects our body, mind, spirit, and heart in order to respond compassionately to something in our life.

First, we reflect with our heart. We identify what we feel without making any judgment about those feelings. We observe what is happening in our life and relationships that might relate to what we are feeling.

Second, we introspect using our logical mind. Again, without judgment, we attempt to understand what is truly amiss. We actively search for patterns of reaction.

Third, we integrate our understanding in ways that shift our fear-filled reactions to compassionate responses. More often than not, we change our thinking or behavior because we see that we were thinking and acting out of preconceptions about our self or others, rather than knowledge and understanding. This process, practiced regularly, transforms us. We become more true to our self, and more compassionate of others.

Use the following questions to reflect, introspect, and integrate transformation into your own life. Enter into a reflective place, where you just notice the many potential answers that reside in your quiet mind. Then engage your introspection.

How do these responses fit with the reality of who you are? Which ones are authentic and which ones challenge your illusions? Next, integrate what you have learned by embracing what is real and true and letting go of the unreal and the untruthful. Let go of the illusion.

- How is your internal monologue drawing your attention?
- Where is your internal monologue occurring? Is it drawing you to the past or the future? Is it firmly rooted in the present?
- What is your reaction or response to the monologue?

- Take a long, loving look at the intent and purpose of the internal monologue.
- Rewrite the script to be a response filled with curious daring.

Part 2

Creating the Spans, Connecting the Pillars

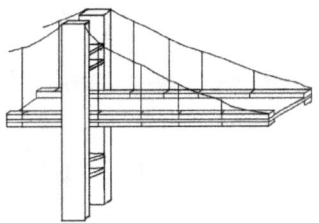

Introduction

Once we lay our foundational awareness by agreeing to cause no harm, alleviating suffering, and taking life as it is, we begin to notice how our actions either reflect this awareness or do not. With curious daring we continue to reflect upon and modify our actions in ways that bring balance to our life and in the world. Our compassionate action is possible because we willingly take an honest, intentional look at our life: we identify what is authentic and courageously change what is not.

As we integrate the four pillars into our daily experiences, we find being present, knowing who we are, living with curious daring, and intentionally looking at our life becomes second nature. As the four pillars sink into our foundational awareness and the seven elements support each other, the easier it becomes to complete our compassion bridge by building the spans and laying the deck that connect the pillars.

Our bridge's walking deck is built from our thoughts, words, and actions. Each interaction is presented as a tile on the bridge's deck. The building of the deck is supported by our awareness in the present moment. Through this awareness we sustain the silence of our quiet mind. With the internal monologue in our quiet mind we connect authentically to others.

Our internal monologue is the source of our interactions and serves as the ground of our relationships with our self, others, the Sacred, and all of creation. We nurture our relationships through our intuitive and compassionate responses. We damage them with each fear-filled reaction. Our responses and reactions are generated by our views, perceptions, and judgments of the world.

When we use certain life tools, we see more clearly the impact of our reactions and responses. One such tool of enlightenment is the Seven Gifts of the Spirit. Incorporating the Seven Gifts of the Spirit into our life nurtures compassionate responses and diminishes fear-filled reactions. The Seven Gifts of the Spirit, found in the Bible (Isaiah 11: 1-10), are guides that encourage a loving, compassionate view of the world.

These gifts are knowledge, understanding, wisdom, courage, right judgment, reverence, and wonder/awe. We gather knowledge in order to gain understanding. By consciously seeking to understand, we gain wisdom. Courage, coupled with wisdom, empowers us to make right judgments. With each right judgment, we show deep respect in all our relationships. Deep, profound respect is reverence. Reverence is the light that brightly illuminates the wonder and awe of this world.

When we receive and use these gifts, we strengthen our discernment of reality. Our personal reality is a mixture of truths, half-truths, and falsehoods. We work to sort through them and filter the authentic from the illusory. They allow us to identify the Sacred in our life and strengthen the connection between our intent and compassionate action.

Without a strong sense of our true self we would be lost amidst our myriad illusions. It would be difficult if not impossible to discern the difference between what is real and what is false. Courageously, we sift through all our illusions to discover our authentic nature. When we find more aspects of our true self, we realize that we are not born to be solitary. We are created to thrive in the connectivity of relationships. We seek more than community; we seek communion. This desire for this deeper connection compels us to build our life bridge.

We build the spans of our bridge through formal contemplative practices and other compassion-centric tools that draw our attention to the sacred manifest in the present moment. Formal contemplative practices include meditation, yoga, tai chi, and journaling. Using formal contemplative practices we establish a daily routine to expand the silence in our quiet mind and increase our capacity to be aware in the moment.

Introduction

We may also employ tools to expand this awareness. One such tool is our breath — something we are never without. We easily attend to the cadence of our breathing as a way to bring our awareness into the present moment. Such practices and tools of contemplation, along with the Seven Gifts of the Spirit, assist us in building our bridge of engaged compassion. In the mindful silence created through these tools we grow more aware of our intent to act in compassionate ways.

Chapter 4

The Gifts of the Spirit: Seven Compassionate Guides

I began my adult journey with the seven gifts just over twenty years ago. As a staff member of a retreat center, I led retreats for young people preparing for the sacrament of Confirmation. A person making a commitment to his/her faith receives an anointing and is graced with the Holy Spirit. The retreats focused on the Seven Gifts of the Spirit and their practical integration into each person's life. In the intervening years, I have returned again and again to those moments of retreat preparation. Each time I have re-discovered an ever deeper and more personal way to incorporate the gifts into my authentic being.

Any one of us can embrace the spiritual gifts that serve as compassionate guides for our journey. They may be identified in The Book of Isaiah, Chapter 10, of the Old Testament; however, such gifts are not solely for followers of Judaism and Christianity. Our divine spark, a bit of the Sacred, lives within us all. The Seven Gifts of the Spirit channeling through our divine spark, connect us to a richer, more compassion filled life. As we commit to living compassionately with deep awareness and curious daring, we begin to recognize the action of these gifts in our life. Knowledge, understanding, wisdom, courage, right judgment, reverence, and wonder/awe are the Seven Gifts of the Spirit.

Imagine a beautiful staircase winding upwards. Seven risers, seven gifts, each one moving us higher up the stairs that leads to the deck of our bridge. By the top of the staircase, we are hyperaware of the gentle power of these gifts and their profound influence in our life. Each in its way deepens our ability to act with intent. They assist and guide our efforts to be compassionate in every step of the way.

Once we learn about the gifts and our actions begin to reflect them, we are better able to discern whether our intent is sincere and actions are compassionate. Not all of our intent is pure or our actions helpful. Through the seven gifts, we gain a contemplative perspective, which may be different than our current one. When the two perspectives and the resulting actions differ, we have a choice: we can continue the hurtful behavior or we can trust the Spirit to guide us to a place of compassionate response.

As we make this choice, we may be guided by one gift in particular or several gifts at the same time. It is through contemplation that we intuitively know which gifts we are called to use and how we can optimally incorporate the gifts into our lives. To begin this journey with the gifts we step upon the first riser of the spiral staircase, knowledge. With this guide we gather information about our self, the world, and our place in the world.

The First Compassionate Guide: Knowledge

From the time we enter this world we are bombarded with information. As infants we have no filters with which to screen the information. In these first moments of life, we unintentionally absorb all stimuli. It is only over time that we develop a filter to screen out what does not appear to be useful to us. Then we look at what remains after the filtering and sort through it to better understand our life patterns and triggers.

Living in the electronic age, we can literally gain knowledge about anything at any time. We have access to information any moment of any day. We must have a certain level of awareness in order to resist information overload. Only through the intentional use of our filters do we safeguard the silence of our quiet mind.

The Gifts of the Spirit: Seven Compassionate Guides

Of course, we must regularly check our filters to ensure that they are not obstructing the flow of information that we need to be compassionate. We do not want our filters to block or hinder us from discovering the illusions we hold about our self and the world. We value the gift of knowledge.

We allow our filters to regulate the flow of information and knowledge. We begin to make judgments and assumptions about what we learn. As our knowledge base grows so does our capacity for informed action. What we learn might be practical, such as survival or social skills, or metaphysical, such as how to thrive in this world. Regardless, the gift of knowledge spurs us to explore the world's great treasure-filled landscape.

The gift of knowledge activates our curious daring. We push past the boundaries of our insular world. Our great quest is to learn and to absorb as much knowledge as possible about our self and the world around us.

Through this gift, we form our personal reality. Knowledge broadens our worldview and anchors us in the real. What is learned through this gift forms the foundation through which the other gifts impact our personal reality.

The first step onto the spiral staircase, knowledge, begins and continues the great quest to learn about our self, others, and the world. This quest is accomplished with an open mind and curious daring. We open our self to gaining knowledge for knowledge's sake. Although the knowledge we learn may validate our view of life, it can just as easily negate judgments and assumptions we had believed were true.

The keys to gaining knowledge are being non-judgmental and non-attached to any particular view or idea. Our sole goal is information gathering. We do not study, analyze, or draw conclusions. We simply gather information, and, with the knowledge gained, we position our self to use the next gift — understanding.

The Second Compassionate Guide: Understanding

As we increase our knowledge base through information gathering, we ask questions, draw conclusions, and make assumptions and judgments. Our questions, conclusions, assumptions, and judgments are our attempts to understand the information we gain. We notice whether the new information confirms our authentic self or mires us in illusion. Not all information is leads to authentic understanding.

We now need to discern whether what we are learning is aligned with our intent to live compassionately. Coming to understanding involves discerning the value of the knowledge we hold. It requires two levels of awareness. First, we are aware how we interpret new information through our internal monologue. Second, we turn our awareness outward to understand how others are interpreting the same information. Understanding encourages us to weigh what we learn and how we may be filtering that knowledge. This spiritual gift helps us to discover what is most true and not simply based on our own or others' assumptions and judgments.

Understanding calls for us to be in the present moment as we identify our biases, judgments, and assumptions. Through this real-time awareness, we recognize our filters and realize we process and understand all information through them. With curious daring, we examine our filters to identify which are reliable and which are faulty. Only then can we understand how our filters help or hinder our understanding.

As we strengthen or reframe our understanding, we question our judgments and challenge our beliefs with curious daring. In these moments of challenging and questioning, we gain opportunities to create a truer, more accurate reality and life vision. No longer do we need to stay firmly entrenched in the illusions of our personal reality. Instead, we are open to seeing the world in a new way.

The spiritual gift of understanding is like a light switch. When flipped on, the shadows disappear, and we understand with clarity why we perceive the world as we do. Understanding creates new ways of perceiving and responding to the world around us. We engage in a compassionate co-existence by seeking to understand the stance of another. Through understanding we realize why two people are reacting or responding differently to the same knowledge.

We realize that we tend to trust information sources that strengthen our own judgments and assumptions whether or not they are biased. We may automatically discredit other sources if they challenge our judgments and assumptions. The spiritual gift of understanding helps us identify and let go of our biases and attachments.

As we practice non-attached understanding, we acknowledge our snap judgments and avoid drawing hasty conclusions. Spiritual understanding is not useful in defending false judgments and assumptions; it will only serve to light the way to the truth. In truth we strive to understand even what might shake our very foundation. Understanding is non-defensive and non-judgmental at its heart. This gift invites us to reform our personal reality.

Our assumptions and judgments are not us, and we should not use them as a basis for self-judging. That is key. Understanding invites us into a place of wide openness, acceptance, and compassion — first for our self and then for those around us, whatever their assumptions and judgments.

Practicing awareness in the moment allows us to grow in understanding, which is an immense gift we can unwrap only one layer at a time. As we gain information from others through our interactions with them — in conversation, reading, watching TV, surfing the web — we strive to never lose contact with our internal monologue. We can always listen with the ear of our heart to our internal monologue. This inner conversation may either enhance our understanding of others or provide a barrier to that understanding. We are conscious not to negate or validate knowledge in way that prevent or strengthen an accurate understanding. These new perceptions stretch our reality and increase our self awareness. For example, we struggle to understand what is going on in some interactions. During those times we might find that we are not listening clearly to our internal monologue.

Understanding calls us to embrace the rhythms of our relationships. When the rhythm is choppy and the relationship strained, we can use our understanding to respond to and alleviate that suffering. Understanding guides us to act in loving, gentle ways instead of in ways that are hurtful and closed. While the gift of understanding is inner focused, it forms the base for our interactions in the external world. Many violent acts are based on misunderstandings or by drawing premature conclusions. The gift of understanding invites us to examine the information, see if it is incomplete, and do more fact finding to gain a clearer picture.

Peoples' understandings of the same information may differ. The spirit of understanding does not always broker an agreement, but it does help us to realize how the other person came to their understanding. Using this gift requires that we enter into dialogue with others in order to resolve confusion and conflicts in order to promote understanding of the other's personal reality.

This understanding does not guarantee we will reach a consensus or even a compromise. Sometimes there may be little common ground on which to build consensus. However, intentional understanding leads us to know the other in non-superficial, compassionate, holistic ways. This under- standing prompts us to breathe deeply and take the next step up the staircase. There we greet the third Gift of the Spirit, wisdom.

The Third Compassionate Guide: Wisdom

Knowledge gained and understood brings us to the third riser on the staircase of gifts, wisdom. Through understanding, we become aware that the communal worldview encompasses more than our own personal view. Seeking to understand the world without using the filter through which we gain our preconceived notions means engaging curious daring. We do not seek to understand in order to negate. Rather, we engage our wise heart and enter

The Gifts of the Spirit: Seven Compassionate Guides 71

into respectful discourse. Such dialogue challenges us to be authentic. Wisdom verifies what is true in our perception and casts light on what is not. Wisdom gives us the grace to acknowledge that our way may not be the only or best way.

As we mature, gain additional knowledge, and seek to understand our self and others, wisdom grows. Courageously choosing to engage wisdom over our self-interests, we question our assumptions, examine our judgments, and open ourselves to myriad possibilities. Wisdom allows us to balance our beliefs with those of others for the sake of others. The gift of wisdom helps us to be non-defensive. Wisdom is not smugness; it is humility. We are non-attached and non-judgmental. Wisdom helps us to acknowledge our vulnerability and let down our guard. We become intimately connected with others.

Living from the 4nons — non-attachment, non-judgment, non-defensiveness, and non-violence — provides fertile ground for wisdom to grow. We grow in wisdom when we question our judgments and beliefs. The first two Gifts of the Spirit, knowledge and understanding, help us to let go of any preconceptions or desires we have that are untrue or inauthentic. With the gift of wisdom; however, we begin a paradigm shift and discover a much more authentic reality.

Non-judgment means living with humility while being intensely aware of our own beliefs and preferences. Through this way of being we recognize the judgments and assumptions that inform our everyday decisions are often not made consciously. Being non-judgmental does not mean negating our own judgments and assumptions; rather, it means deciding not to react when they are challenged by someone else's judgments or assumptions. When we are non-judgmental, we respond from a place of wise openness, instead of from a place of insecurity or fear.

A non-defensive attitude invites us to recognize others without feeling the need to explain, excuse, or justify our beliefs. Right, wrong, or indifferent, our assumptions and judgments are ours and form our reality. We may "own who we are" without being defensive or making excuses or laying blame on anyone else. Wisdom shines light on the path ahead of us and illuminates growth opportunities. We transform our life by releasing ideas or patterns of thinking that no longer serve us. If we are wise, we are open. The benefits of this gift outweigh the risks.

Still, we may feel vulnerable when we let our guard down. For many, the world and other people seem quite threatening. As we have discussed, the level of violence in the world is heartbreaking. And, we have all been touched by violence in one way or another. With wisdom we rewrite our thoughts and navigate to a less violent reality using our words and actions.

When most people speak of violence, they are talking about acts of heinous violence they hear about in the news. We tend to ignore the violence we turn inward, and the damage and harm we perpetrate on our self. We may also be unaware of how we project inward violence outward onto others. Taking a non-violent stance requires us to attend to our thoughts as well as our words and actions. We need to be hyperaware of our violent thoughts and consider how someone might be hurt by the words and actions that result from them. Through courage, the next gift, we live openly despite the risks.

The Fourth Compassionate Guide: Courage

Having courage does not mean lacking fear. No, courage comes with the understanding that there is plenty to fear. That same wisdom propels us to work through fear. We need to find ways to respond despite our fears because wise action is only possible with courage.

Fear is a constant companion on our quest for knowledge and understanding. Irrational fears lurk in our subconscious and rise unbidden to our conscious mind. Often we cannot wrap our mind around a fear for which there seems to be no rational reason for it. For example, I have a fear of heights. While my phobia has diminished over my lifetime, it is still palpable. Sometimes, when I am too high, I can taste the thickness of this fear. No matter how much knowledge, understanding, or wisdom I have in reserve, the fear still paralyzes me. Through the gift of courage, I wisely accept my limitation.

Courage will not always help us do what we set out to. It will not help us stand bravely as we make thoughtless decisions that hurt others. No, the gift of courage is not a slayer of all that ails us, nor is it a coolant for the heat of the moment. It is truly a sibling to the first three gifts, knowledge, understanding, and wisdom. Those are what it valiantly protects for us. Only through courage do we engage our own curious daring and Divine Spark. It warms our compassionate spirit. In my case, it prompted me to take life as it is. I will have to courageously deal with my fear of heights for the foreseeable future.

So we have climbed the first four steps of the staircase and invited four of the seven Gifts of the Spirit into our life. While we may feel fear, we understand from the gift of courage that we do not always have to react to our fears. If the reaction persists, that is okay. Life is not perfect. Sometimes it is messy and produces fear. Courage is the acknowledgment that life is what it is. We do the best we can in the moment to navigate fear on our life journey.

Courage, like the other guides, calls us to examine our assumptions, listen to our internal monologue, and to use wisdom to discover our truth. Courage coupled with wisdom invites us to change or gives us the security to stay where we are. When we act with courage, we act with curious daring. We engage compassion through the next gift, right judgment.

The Fifth Compassionate Guide: Right Judgment

Judgment is not a bad word. In each moment of every day, we make judgments. We are not even aware of many of them. Some are mundane, like deciding what street is best to take to work. Others are more significant: for example, judging what is "best" for our children after a divorce or whether to begin or end a relationship. These are just a very few of the many judgments we make every day.

Judgments may seem to be spur of the moment decisions, but in reality, most of our judgments are based upon certain assumptions we have made based upon our past experiences. They are only detrimental if they form the basis for reactive behavior that causes harm. When we understand what lies at the root of the judgment, we can determine if it is necessary for our authentic expression of self. With wisdom and courage we can redress any judgment that has been hurtful or triggered reactive behavior. We can rescript or nullify any judgments and assumptions that foster illusion and cause suffering.

Right judgment is the basis of our compassionate response to life. We do not react when engaging in right judgment. Coming to this place of right judgment requires a certain mastery of the first four gifts. Right judgment is a response based upon both knowledge of and an understanding of our views and personal reality. Once we gain clarity, we look at those who may have impacted by our illusions. Wisdom offers a way to compensate for our past acts. Through courage we exercise right judgment and transform to a more authentic person.

When we are present in the moment, we are aware of the dance between our inner monologue and our external dialogue. Our external dialogue includes not only conversations with others but everything we sense in our environment — even the background noise. The process of making a right judgment occurs when we are aware of the assumptions in our monologue and how they directly impact our external dialogue. Practicing right judgment requires vigilance. We are aware which of our assumptions might trigger a reaction externally while we formulate a response internally. The gift of right judgment assists us with real-time discernment as needed.

When we discern, guided by judgment, we are not attached to a chosen outcome. We are open to securing the best outcome. Through deep reflection and introspection, we choose what is best regardless of how it may impact us. Discernment requires that we courageously come to a right judgment based upon knowledge gained, understanding earned, and wisdom applied. Discernment requires that we humbly accept our wisdom and show reverence as we make right judgment.

The Sixth Compassionate Guide: Reverence

Respect is honoring someone for the person they are as well as what they do. We might respect a person's actions and words and the good influence they have on others. We respect those with integrity, those whom we trust. We want to respect others and have them respect us.

Reverence is a deep form of respect. When we feel reverence, we are fully engaged in honoring the other. Not only is our heart moved by the other, our mind and spirit are moved too. The spiritual gift of reverence connects us to others and the world on ever deepening levels. Reverence is cherishing another simply because they are a part of creation, not because of what they have done. Reverence is not fleeting; it cannot be withdrawn. It is a profound, wordless connection to another.

We show reverence when are aware of how our actions, thoughts, and words impact others. We acknowledge when we slip and show disrespect. We are filled with joy when we are able to halt any harm before it begins. Right judgment and courage are needed when we forget to show reverence to another, and it is necessary to make amends. The gift of reverence infuses our simple acts of compassion with abiding love.

Sharing reverence is more profound than feeling respect for another person; however, being respectful is this gift's foundation. When we feel reverence, our respect becomes deeper than an intellectual or cognitive response. What we feel is a heart-centered emotion. It flows from our spirit, and we feel it in our body, mind, and heart. Reverence is a way of being.

When our reverent spirit is engaged, we connect with the world in incredible ways. Our stance is loose, free, and open. We see the world optimistically. We see the intrinsic potential of all, including our self. Reverence invites us to embrace our world with wonder and awe.

The Seventh Compassionate Guide: Wonder and Awe

As a child we looked at the world around us with wonder and awe. We were enraptured. Would not it be wonderful to see the world that way again? I am often amazed and a bit envious when someone sees beyond the grime and discouragement of the world and talks about a bright world filled with possibilities. How amazing it would be to explore those possibilities moment by moment!

The spiritual gift of wonder and awe is not simply a passive appreciation for what is good or right in our world; rather, it is the being fully alive and full of grace. It is the culmination of every gift. It embraces and fulfills us. When we live each moment filled with the grace inherent in our being and in each particle of the world, we are suffused with the awe-inspiring wonder of our world. This awareness is the basis of our life work. Wonder and awe nourish our compassionate intent and the spirit our compassionate action.

Learning about the Seven Gifts of the Spirit is the first step. The next are taken with these companion guides. We must never forget that we live in the present and must choose how to respond, moment by moment. We are the architect, the builder, and the interior decorator of our present moment. Knowing that there is much we do not and may never understand about life shouldn't discourage us. We have the guidance we need to see beyond the superficial and delve deeply into the unknown. While we do not know what resides in the cool depths of this unknown, we may shelter there safe in wonder and awe of the Sacred.

The Gifts of the Spirit are willing guides for people seeking to engage compassion through intent and action. The gifts are in many ways "custom-made" for those making that journey. Because we must start somewhere, we begin with knowledge. If we do not have a knowledge base, we lack the information to begin to ask the questions that lead to understanding. When we gain understanding, we have a clearer view of what other questions we need to ask. Wisdom can only be gained and shared through our understanding, our continued quest for knowledge, and our awareness of our perceptions.

The Gifts of the Spirit: Seven Compassionate Guides

These three gifts, knowledge, understanding, and wisdom are the foundation of our personal reality. We live from our reality by courageously making right judgments. Through right judgment we show reverence. With right judgment comes the desire to act upon our understanding from a place of deep reverence. Reverence opens the eyes of our heart, mind, spirit, and body. We see with our entire being the wonder and awe in us and in our world. We are continually surprised by unexpected opportunities to share compassion.

Intent & Action: Meditating on the Seven Gifts

By gaining knowledge and intending to learn from it,
  I grow in understanding
By seeking to understand before being understood,
  I gain wisdom
By accepting the challenge of wisdom,
  I formulate right judgment
By making right judgment,
  I embrace the courage to be authentic
By acting with courage,
  I show reverence to myself and all the world
By intending reverence, compassion shines through all I am
  I am filled with the wonder and awe of the Sacred.
The wonder and awe of the Sacred continually inspires me.

RI²: Reflection, Introspection, & Integration

RI² is a contemplative practice that connects our body, mind, spirit, and heart in order to respond compassionately to something in our life.

First, we reflect with our heart. We identify what we feel without making any judgment about those feelings. We observe what is happening in our life and relationships that might relate to what we are feeling.

Second, we introspect using our logical mind. Again, without judgment, we attempt to understand what is truly amiss. We actively search for patterns of reaction.

Third, we integrate our understanding in ways that shift our fear-filled reactions to compassionate responses. More often than not, we change our thinking or behavior because we see that we were thinking and acting out of preconceptions about our self or others, rather than knowledge and understanding. This process, practiced regularly, transforms us. We become more true to our self, and more compassionate of others.

Use the following questions to reflect, introspect, and integrate transformation into your own life. Enter into a reflective place, where you just notice the many potential answers that reside in your quiet mind. Then engage your introspection. How do these responses fit with the reality of who you are? Which ones are authentic and which ones challenge your illusions? Next, integrate what you have learned by embracing what is real and true and letting go of the unreal and the untruthful. Let go of the illusion.

Sit quietly and recall a judgment or an assumption that you made during the course of the past several days. Use the seven gifts to understand that judgment in light of your current awareness.

- What knowledge has led to your understanding of this belief?
- What additional knowledge would lead to greater understanding? Resolve to gain that knowledge and revisit your understanding.
- Has your judgment or assumption shifted?
- How did refining your understanding with wisdom and courage encourage that shift?
- If you have shifted your judgment, how is that coloring your reverence for the person or situation you were judging?
- Notice how this shift also stimulates your wonder and awe in the world.

Chapter 5

Drawing Our Attention to the Present: Contemplative Practice

Living compassionately begins with our intent to be compassionate and culminates in each compassionate act. But, we all know which road is paved with good intentions. We do not want that road to be our bridge's deck. While it is our intention to be compassionate, often our actions are anything but compassionate. How can we be sure to do what we intend – to live compassionately?

Being present in the moment and ever aware of our compassionate intent helps us to pave our deck with authentic acts of compassion. By believing that compassion is the only response to the world around us, we continually seek opportunities to act compassionately. Contemplative practice trains us to remain mindful. It reminds us that our first intention is to do no harm. Contemplative practice creates and sustains an environment in which our compassionate intent flourishes and becomes compassionate action.

Contemplative practices connect us to our foundational awareness — the three agreements. They also help us to engage the four pillars on which our compassion bridge rests. Contemplative practices are a like the cables of a suspension bridge, which absorb physical stresses and help to maintain a bridge's integrity. Likewise, contemplation helps us to handle the stresses in our life and to stay focused on compassionate intent. Contemplation is simply being present to the moment fully aware of our life unfolding. Only in the present moment can we actively engage intent.

Contemplative practice exists in many secular and spiritual forms. For me, a contemplative practice is any experience that fosters the silence in our quiet mind, stimulates our hyperawareness, and focuses our attention on the present moment. Through contemplative practices, we expand our understanding of our self, our relationships, and our engagement with the world.

Such practices reveal the integrity of the filters through which we view reality and our illusions. By engaging in the practices we listen to our internal monologue and determine whether it represents our authentic self. We come to understand what makes us defensive rather than authentic. By practicing mindfulness regularly, we more confidently shift from fear-filled reaction to compassionate response. When we become aware of our emotional triggers, we can choose to respond rather than react. Both internally and outwardly we become poised to intuitively respond in loving, gentle ways. We are able to engage compassion through our intent and action.

A routine of contemplative practice helps us to cultivate inner silence. Within this environment of silence our quiet mind flourishes. Clarity is only possible within the silence of our quiet mind. We are aware when our internal monologue, our real-time thoughts, are less than compassionate. By focusing on the unfolding moment, we have less energy to expend on past worries and future concerns.

All of our energy is focused on what is happening now. This powers our choice to respond compassionately in the moment. Regular, engaged awareness calms our spirit and strengthens its connection to our mind, body, and heart. A quiet serenity flows into our everyday life.

This overflow of peace creates a compassion centric rhythm in our life. This rhythm created by contemplative practice benefits us in the moment and may have a far-reaching, positive impact on the world. If chaos theory hypothesizes that the fluttering of a butterfly's wings in China can trigger a hurricane in the Western

Hemisphere, is not it just as possible that one compassionate act born from our sincere intent might ripple across the globe transforming lives?

Studies have been undertaken on specific contemplative practices like Tai Chi and meditation. These studies show that the regular practice of Tai Chi increases concentration and focus as well as mobility and agility. Brain scans of people who meditate regularly show higher than average neural activity in certain areas of the brain. Such a shift in brain chemistry seems to reduce stress, increase focus, and encourage empathy. The physical benefits of meditation inevitably increase our response flexibility.

Through a regular practice, we are better able to make choices without angst and in ways that reflect our authentic self. Other contemplative practices may not have been studied in the same way. Yet, from personal experience, I know that many others I incorporate into my routine benefit me.

Our quiet mind is opened through regular contemplative practice. With this open mind comes clarity. Through this clear seeing we are better able to recognize our illusions and their roots: our assumptions and judgments. Those illusions create the roles we play, our superficial persona. We grow when we begin to question the authenticity of those personas and the realities they help to create.

Through contemplative practice, we explore our personal reality and discover our authentic self. We challenge the illusions, one by one, as we identify them. The awareness from our contemplation migrates into our life. We begin to notice the disconnects: when what we say or do is not mindful or true to our self, but reflects some illusion we have about our self. Contemplative practice strengthens our quiet mind. We release our illusions one by one, grateful to be free of them.

Contemplative practices benefit our physical bodies, our mind, emotional state, and our spiritual being. Although there is no cookie-cutter way to embrace contemplative practice, we are called to experiment, play, and discover the practices that help us most. There is no wrong practice. There are only the practices that provide maximum benefit. It is for us to discern which practices allow our authentic being to surface and respond compassionately to the world. The goal is to enjoy the journey.

Beginners may choose an attitude of playful curiosity when experiencing a contemplative practice. Know that we each pave our compassion bridge's deck one span at a time, with what we learn as we practice mindfulness. If one contemplative practice does not resonate after a while, we choose to explore other practices until we discover one that aligns with the silence in our quiet mind and increases our awareness.

Over the years, I have enjoyed the contemplative practices of journaling, walking, mindful breathing, and Tai Chi. When I have an opportunity to walk a labyrinth, I do. One practice that I still find difficult is sitting meditation. That being said, I regularly try sitting meditation, to see if the time is right for sitting meditation to enhance my environment of silence. We never know what we may discover as we practice.

Contemplative practices can and do change us. I have always been fascinated with labyrinths. A true labyrinth has one entrance and one winding path to the center. Prior to my walking through one for the first time, some colleagues expressed concern that I would not be able to slow down enough to walk this path in mindful meditation. I entered the labyrinth with curious daring. The twists and turns in the path forced me to slow down. Walking the labyrinth was a wonderful, calming, quieting experience for me. As I moved deeper into the labyrinth, I connected with my quiet mind and became hyperaware of the stillness both within and without.

Since then, each time I walk the labyrinth I find a beautiful message waiting for me in the middle of the labyrinth. If I had listened to the voices of concern and not attempted walking the labyrinth, I would not have reaped the benefits of contemplative practice of labyrinth walking.

Life is a great adventure, which can only be enjoyed if we are aware. As we explore and experience contemplative practices, we find amazing treasures that strengthen our authentic self and support an engaged, eager response to life as it is in all its wonder. When we approach contemplative practice with curious daring and eager anticipation, we cannot fail. The practices are meant to be explored, to be experienced, and to be modified to fit our unique contemplative nature. Through this process we fine-tune our intent, and our compassion bursts forth.

Intent & Action: Contemplation: Not a Cookie-Cutter Practice

In the past twenty years, I have attended a number of workshops and retreats on a variety of contemplative practices. Often my expectations fell short, and I found myself frustrated by my perceived failure — my inability to engage the practice and enter into the clarity of my quiet mind. I had been journaling since my early teens, so imagine my dismay during one workshop when the leader informed me that I had been journaling in the wrong way.

That journaling incident was the beginning of the transition of my perception concerning contemplative practice. At about the same time, I happened upon several books that highlighted different ways of journaling. My internal monologue questioned how any one of those ways could be THE way. I began to experiment with different contemplative practices while listening to my quiet mind. I continued to practice what engaged me and left what did not work for me. With curious daring, I tried different practices, with the caveat that I not feel compelled to do anything that did not resonate with my spirit. I also refused to allow my internal monologue to label me a failure.

Contemplative practices stimulate hyperawareness of our judgments and assumptions. They shine a bright light on our illusions. We attend to our internal monologue and are mindful of opportunities to shift our reactions to responses. Within the silence of our quiet mind, we birth the courage to challenge our assumptions and judgments. Through contemplative practice, the courage is found to begin our personal transformation.

What contemplative practices may be better suited for you? Respondents of The Merton Institute for Contemplative Living's

2012 survey reported using a wide variety of contemplative practices. The following sampling of some of the practices may engage your contemplative spirit.

The Merton Institute for Contemplative Living was a non-profit organization that dissolved in December 2012. Its mission was to deepen the understanding of contemplative living through the works of Thomas Merton. The survey was undertaken in the Summer of 2012.

Meditation

Ask ten people what form of mediation they practice, and you may receive eleven different answers. All forms of meditation have a common purpose: to strengthen the silence of our quiet mind. Within this environment of silence rests the clarity of our quiet mind. The silence allows us to avoid our distractions, clearly hear our internal monologue, and release our desire to react.

Formal sitting meditation is an invitation to rest silently and connect with our quiet mind. During a session, we are aware of our internal monologue and intentionally release any thoughts, feelings, and sensations that arise. Through meditation we train our quiet mind to focus on the present moment and release the thoughts that are agitating. We rest within the Sacred, the still, while not being distracted by our quiet voice.

Whatever helps us to connect with the silence within us, with a quiet, peace-filled mind, is a good practice for us. Some people prefer to meditate while walking rather than sitting. A meditative walk allows us to physically journey down a path as a means of clearing our mind. It may also help us to repeat a word, a mantra, or focus on our breath, when we meditate. Some use a lit candle or image called a yantra to help them focus on the present moment and still their mind. The point is not to keep our attention on that word or our breath or an image or our footfalls. These things simply bring our attention to the present moment, make us aware of our distraction, and prevent the loss of focus on the present moment.

Drawing Our Attention to the Present: Contemplative Practice

Whatever form of meditation we choose, the attitude we cultivate during the practice is important. We intend for our quiet mind to be suffused with silence and open to grace. Grace, for me, is a intangible gift that fills me with the ability to rest in the quiet moment. When meditating we are filled with grace, our divine spark is ignited, and we rest within the Sacred.

The goal of meditation is not to rest mentally in a place of silence where no words flit across our mind. The goal of meditation is to create an environment of silence within our quiet mind. Within the silence, we train our quiet mind to respond to our internal monologue instead of reacting from it. The ultimate goal of meditation, and our life, is to grow in compassion.

Practicing meditation fosters the clarity of hearing we need in order to be aware of our internal monologue and the Sacred within. We bring this new awareness into our encounters with others. Meditation may fill us with a lightness of being and a joy, which reminds us of the unconditional love we seek to share.

Movement

Running, walking, biking, swimming — exercise is vital to our physical health. It is also beneficial to our emotional, mental, and spiritual health. Aerobic exercise releases endorphins that produce feelings of wellbeing and elevate our mood. By engaging in physical activity, we disconnect from our thoughts and better respond to our internal monologue. The movement of our body is a physical mantra that moves us into the silence within. We disconnect from our thoughts and connect to the silence our quiet mind with the rhythm of our body.

Dance is another physical way of releasing our thoughts. We either follow a pattern or move freely to the music. By focusing on our steps, we totally engage in the present moment. Although we anticipate the next step, we trust that our feet, and the rest of our body, know where to go. In this way, dance is wordless meditation.

Other physical forms of meditation are Tai Chi and yoga. Both involve a series of poses that invite us to synchronize our movement with our breath. We perform certain movements with an inhale, others with an exhale. As we move and breathe in tandem, we consciously connect with our body, mind, spirit, and heart as we move. We follow what feels like a sacred rhythm, one that connects us to the greater community. Through movement we have engaged compassion. We have strengthened our relationship with our self, with the Sacred, with others, with all of creation.

Creativity

Contemplative practice is defined as an experience that fosters our quiet mind, provides a gateway to a state of hyperawareness, and focuses our attention on the present moment. Any activity that engages our creativity are easily incorporated into our contemplative practice. The creative arts certainly do all of that.

My creative outlet is writing. When I put pen to paper, I often lose myself as the words pour out onto the paper. In that moment of total engagement, my hand picks up cues from my mind, heart, and spirit. My uncensored, authentic self flows into my writing. It does not matter if I am journaling or writing a blog or book chapter; writing is a contemplative experience that engages my whole person.

Writing, for me, is contemplative and therapeutic. As the words from my mind, heart, and spirit are written, I release unsavory or unsettling emotions or thoughts. Their toxic residue dissipates, and I gain fresh perspective. Once this toxic resonance is no longer clanging inside of me, I can take a long, loving look at what is real. Engaging the 4nons, I read what I have written. I am non-attached to the feeling triggered by the words; I do not judge the emotions behind the word. I am not defensive about what triggered the thought or feeling. I commit to a non-violent response as I read. By writing, I effectively acknowledge my soul angst and invite my self to rest in a sea of compassion. This creative process has been transformative in my life.

Drawing Our Attention to the Present: Contemplative Practice

To see through the eyes of an artist and to create our heart vision with our hands is truly amazing. Art invites us to see the world differently, to see the beauty in both the certain and the uncertain. Visual art that we create may reveal the beauty of something that once seemed uninteresting or even ugly. Now when I look at the photo of a worried, worn person, I no longer see the wrinkles of clothes and skin. I see the beauty and integrity of the spirit that shines within. Photography invites me to step outside my illusions and open my eyes to see what is really there. Any act of creation invites us to step outside of our illusions, embrace our authentic self, and stand firmly in the moment.

We may create fine art, or we may be skilled at a craft. No matter what medium we use, the goal is to rest quietly the world and respond to its beauty. That is the goal of any contemplative practice. Through practice we uncover what is real and reflect that reality authentically in our compassionate action.

Art created as part of our contemplative practice, may feel subtly different to us. What we create may have a resonance, an energy signature that we recognize as having come from a deeper place within us. Sensing this difference, we eagerly engage the contemplative practice again hoping to go deeper still. Art as a contemplation practice may reveal images or ideas we want to explore further.

All of us are artists. Each day we are given a fresh canvas on which to paint our own moment-by-moment experiences. Through contemplation we engage ever more deeply our awareness of our self and the world around us. We might start by sketching the contours of our picture, freely, without much concern. What we discover engages, and we want to fill in the details. Whether our creation is artistic or contemplative — it is uniquely ours and invites us to celebrate life and grow in compassion.

Joyful Noise

We are resonance and sound. Our atoms begin the movement and our molecules and tissues respond. We respond to others with our full body as we pick up their physical, mental, emotional, and spiritual vibrations. What does vibrating matter have to do with contemplation? More than we might realize. Audible and inaudible sounds can either help us to focus our attention or distract us.

Sound can affect our mood and our mental state. Certain sounds, certain music, for example, may foster the silence in our quiet mind; other sounds serve as disrupting distractions. Further, we may listen to music that calmed us yesterday and find that it agitates us today. As with all contemplative practices, our ability to enter into the silence depends upon many factors: some are tangible, others are intangible, but all are sensory.

Chanting and listening to others chant are contemplative practices used in many traditions. For example, Christian monks usually chant in Latin, Buddhist monks in Tibetan. Members of the Jewish community use Hebrew in their prayers. When we do not understand the words, we resonate with the sound. We become absorbed by the chant's rhythm and cadence. We may even be able to meditate better.

Chants are generally intoned in the bass range of the musical scale. Bass sounds resonate within our sacral area, below our diaphragm, near our navel. At times, we might feel that the chant's sound gently reaches into our physical core to free and to ground us. As our core's resonance aligns with the chant's vibration we might literally feel fire in our belly, as we become hyperaware and fully open to the Sacred.

Listening to music may bring us into a contemplative awareness whether the music is instrumental or sung. Music invites us to engage in full body listening and helps us to focus on the present moment. The fluid sound of the music may lift us high into the stratosphere of the spirit and beyond our physical cares. Some music may invite us into a more reflective silence, while other music may stir us to laugh or dance. When we experience music contemplatively, we gain a greater awareness of life's inner connectivity.

Writings of Spiritual Masters and Sacred Scripture

We live in an age when information on any subject is easy to access. No longer do we need to travel far to borrow books by spiritual masters we want to read. Now, thanks to the Internet, most spiritual writings and all of Sacred Scripture is literally at our fingertips.

We can search, find, and with one click order printed, digital, or audio versions of almost anything we want. While choosing what to read might be anything but contemplative, the materials available present a vast opportunity to find spiritual masters whose insights resonate with us.

Reading a spiritual work as a contemplative practice does not end when we close the book. The next step is to discern its value to our spiritual journey. The RI^2 process is helpful to this discernment. During reflection, we pay attention to how what we have read resonates with our spirit, noticing without judgment how the words or message trigger a response within us. We rest in this awareness, neither defending our thoughts nor attempting to refute the truth of what we have read. Throughout this period of reflection we remain unattached to what our awareness reveals.

Next, we engage in introspection. We seek to understand our disagreements or acceptance of the spiritual writer's words or philosophy. We may not come to a full knowing or understanding at this stage. We may not have sufficient information about the work or our self at that moment to understand that introspection is ongoing. Through the continued practice of RI^2, we trust that the nuances of our feeling and intuition will be revealed. Questions we might ask as we reflect and introspect include:

> What in the piece calls to my spirit?
> What do I see as truth?
> What is in dissonance with my beliefs?

The conclusions we draw during RI² help us grow spiritually. No matter what we come to understand by applying RI², we realize that neither the spiritual master's beliefs nor ours are wrong. Reflection and introspection using RI² help us formulate our own beliefs without judgment or assignment of right or wrong. Even after we identify our beliefs, we continue to examine them using the same process. Beliefs that served us once may no longer align with our authentic self. The contemplative practice of RI² continually deepens the silence in our quiet mind. We respond to the world around us with increasing awareness and clarity.

Again, we do not have to agree with everything or anything a spiritual master articulates. They speak from their experience; no one is **the** expert when it comes to contemplative living. That does not mean we have to react negatively when others' beliefs do not resonate with our own. Spiritual writings serve us best when they challenge our beliefs. They invite us into spiritual inquiry. During this questioning, we develop a greater understanding of our beliefs in light of another's. As we reflect, we may choose to write down our thoughts or just be with them. We may choose to dialogue with another or a group or be alone with our reflections. That we reflect and introspect upon the words of another is what is important.

Reading the spiritual masters and sacred texts invites us into both reflection and introspection. We reflect with our heart and introspect with our analytical mind. Our authentic self is revealed during this ongoing process. We then integrate what emphasizes our authenticity and release what strengthens our illusions. Sometimes our illusions only become apparent to us when we are prompted to defend them. When we find our self reacting negatively to another's beliefs, that is our invitation to re-engage the RI² process to uncover our illusions.

We may also consider engaging others in our discernment. When I attend a lecture given by a spiritual master or read a spiritual text, I dialogue with other attendees or those whom I know have read the same text. This is an opportunity to share my reflections, gain others' insights, and aid my process of reflection and introspection. I find that dialogue leads me to a more stable integration of the spiritual teaching. Sharing with others is also a form of contemplative practice.

Being in Community

Throughout the day we have multiple opportunities to interact with others, verbally and non-verbally. We may have long, intense conversations or short ones. We may see someone laughing and smile, as if we are in on the joke. Whatever the interaction, each time we communicate with another we have an opportunity to create community.

Many spiritual masters stress the importance of practicing silence in the presence of others. Members of the Trappist community of Gethsemani, where Thomas Merton lived half of his life, practice silence most of their day. This intentional silence is not to prevent communication or quiet every sound. In some ways, it heightens the awareness of sound and its distraction. That is the point. We foster the silence in our quiet mind to better hear the within and the without, so we can better respond in peace-filled, compassionate ways.

Silence must be fostered in the present moment. When we are intentionally in the here and now, we hear our internal monologue clearly and are aware how the words or actions we hear are affecting us in the present. In the silence, we are better able to frame a compassionate response.

When we are not sure what we are hearing through full body listening or unsure of how to respond compassionately, we might seek spiritual direction or counseling. Sometimes another person who shares our intent to grow in compassion and self-awareness can be a helpful guide. Whether we are engaging in one-on-one spiritual direction, counseling, or are a part of an ongoing group interaction, the opportunity to create an intimate relationship exists. Within each intimate relationship lies the seed of a contemplative experience. Every relationship and every encounter present opportunities for a contemplative connection. Being with another allows us to practice listening with the ear of our heart and to respond in creatively com- passionate ways. When we engage the other, we practice our contemplative skills and invite others to explore their contemplative natures.

Ritual

All of us have rituals or actions we perform in prescribed ways. Some are as simple as drinking a cup of morning coffee and sitting quietly before we start the day. Others may be part of our contemplative practice, such as sitting in meditation for 20 minutes with a candle burning or practicing Tai Chi once a week. Still other rituals are communal, ones we perform with others to acknowledge our connection. Family and community rituals are used to celebrate holidays, acknowledge a milestone, or mark a passing. Whatever the reason for the ritual, it creates a space for silence and has the potential to draw us deeply into our quiet mind. Through meaningful ritual we connect to our authentic self.

We might engage in religious rituals such as the Catholic Mass, Buddhist group meditation, or other prayer services. We grow into our authentic self by practicing rituals. They offer us a sense of continuity and provide a sense of security when much of our life seems to be in flux. Some of the rituals we embrace in our childhood we continue to practice throughout our life. Others we embrace later in life. Whether we participate in a ritual once or many times, a contemplative ritual's purpose is to draw us into the moment and focus our awareness.

Whatever practices or steps are involved in a contemplative ritual, they should invite us to enter into the silence of our quiet mind. If the contemplative ritual is communal, it also invites us to a place of connective clarity and shared silence. Here we experience contemplative relationship.

This list of contemplative practices is by no means all-inclusive. The ones presented: meditation, movement, creativity, joyful noise, spiritual writings and scripture, community life, and ritual were those mentioned most often in The Merton Institute survey. A simple Internet search for "contemplative practice" will identify many more. While we each may have a few practices that we engage in regularly, curious daring, the third pillar of our life bridge, invites us to try new practices as well.

Many contemplative practices are solitary ones. When we practice alone, we foster our silence within a stable, secure environment. The more we solitarily foster inner silence, the easier it is to respond from that place of silence when we are with others. Whether we are alone or with others, our inner silence brings clarity to our quiet mind. Within this clarity we are aware of our inner monologue and are better able to focus on the present moment.

Sharing a contemplative practice with others deepens our silence. Communal practice strengthens our ability to be aware of our inner monologue while in the presence of others. This is important, because ultimately it is through relationship that we deepen our connection to self, others, the Sacred, indeed all of creation. When we share a contemplative experience, we have the opportunity to be authentic and discover our illusions in the presence of others.

We are vulnerable when we identify and acknowledge the illusions behind our triggers. Relationships provide us the support of others as we choose to respond instead of react. The next step is to journey beyond the comfortable relationships of our contemplative community to continue to practice what we have learned — to be compassionate presence.

We maintain our awareness and intent to respond in loving, compassionate ways. Interacting with others tests us, stretches our authentic self, and reveals our illusions. Interacting with others we call upon all of our resources to maintain and deepen the silence that fosters our authentic self. Our contemplative practice trains us to remain present and conscious of our quiet mind. There we listen to our internal monologue and discern what is authentic. This awareness empowers us to respond to others with compassion.

Contemplative practice enables the silence to survive and our quiet mind to thrive. Solitary contemplative practice forms an environment of silent and creates access to our quiet mind. While we can practice listening to our internal monologue while alone, the true challenge comes when we are with others who might do or say something that triggers reactions or challenges our beliefs. However, such interactions may be positive for us as well. We step outside of the controlled environment of contemplative practice and use the skills gained in real time situations. The awareness that grows from our contemplative practice guides us to be authentic. The more open and authentic we become, the more open and authentic our relationships are.

Contemplative activities within a group offer opportunities to rest in the silence of our quiet mind, remain aware of our monologue, and respond authentically. Contemplative practice ultimately deepens our intimacy with our self and with others. When we have positive, life-giving connections we know we are engaging compassion through intent and action. We are guaranteeing the integrity of our bridge.

RI^2: *Reflection, Introspection, & Integration*

RI^2 is a contemplative practice that connects our body, mind, spirit, and heart in order to respond compassionately to something in our life.

First, we reflect with our heart. We identify what we feel without making any judgment about those feelings. We observe what is happening in our life and relationships that might relate to what we are feeling.

Second, we introspect using our logical mind. Again, without judgment, we attempt to understand what is truly amiss. We actively search for patterns of reaction.

Third, we integrate our understanding in ways that shift our fear-filled reactions to compassionate responses. More often than not, we change our thinking or behavior because we see that we were thinking and acting out of preconceptions about our self

Drawing Our Attention to the Present: Contemplative Practice

or others, rather than knowledge and understanding. This process, practiced regularly, transforms us. We become more true to our self, and more compassionate of others.

Use the following questions to reflect, introspect, and integrate transformation into your own life. Enter into a reflective place, where you just notice the many potential answers that reside in your quiet mind. Then engage your introspection. How do these responses fit with the reality of who you are? Which ones are authentic and which ones challenge your illusions? Next, integrate what you have learned by embracing what is real and true and letting go of the unreal and the untruthful. Let go of the illusion.

Choose at least one contemplative practice to experience for a week. Set aside time in the morning, at midday, and in the evening in which to practice.

- How was the experience? Describe it holistically, in terms of your body, mind, spirit and heart. How did it affect each?
- When did your formal practice stimulate an informal contemplative practice?
- What were the informal contemplative practices you tried?
- What is different now about how you engage other practices in your life?
- How do your respond to your internal monologue during your practice?
- What, if anything, is different now?

Chapter 6

The Toolbox Found In Our Silence

For any job, any profession, most tasks we have to do, we need tools. Some tools are tangible, like a phone or a computer that we physically tote from place to place. Others, like the ability to add and multiply, we carry within our heads. A third kind of tool we carry in our heart. These tools enable our intent to become compassionate action.

Tools of the heart are the ones that help us enter into silence and engage our quiet mind. The intangible skills or awareness that guide us into the present moment are many. We have already talked about some of them: the quiet mind, being hyperaware, and intuitively responding. Without such tools as these we would not be able to actively participate in the moment. Through these tools we identify both the authentic and the illusory parts of our self.

We need no briefcase or vehicle to tote these tools. They are present within and are activated by our heart-felt intent. We can engage each of them in a moment although we must practice using them for the best results. These heart tools may be used at any time: minding the breath, ninety-second release and recovery, the 4nons, discernment and consensus, recollection, and RI^2. Let us look at each one together.

Minding Our Breath

The most easily accessible tool we use to connect with our quiet mind is our breath. Focusing on the breath firmly grounds us into the silence of our quiet mind and turns our focus to the present moment. We listen to our breath while not attempting to shift it. We merely listen. Through this awareness of the cadence of our breath, we receive much information about our physical, mental, and emotional states. As we breathe, we notice our breath's rhythm. We are mindful of the speed or fluidity of each breath. We feel the air flow into our body and sense our body's response to the inflowing air. As we focus on our breath, it naturally begins to even out, deepen. In this calm, we may become aware of what had hurried our breath or been the source of our stress.

The cadence of our breath is a very good indicator of the level of our stress or calm. Coupling our breathing with visualization helps us to discover what switches are waiting to be flipped — what we are concerned is going to happen that will agitate us. We then are able to identify what is occurring in our mind that might trigger a reaction instead of a response.

To enter more deeply into the calm, we may visualize the path the breath takes on the journey through our body from the time air enters our nose. During this visualization, we notice particular places in the body that are tense or sore. We may deepen our breath to increase the flow of oxygen to cramped muscles. Acknowledging pain or discomfort is the first step to releasing it. Unless we identify what is occurring in our body, we will not know how to solve the issue with compassion. Some of our discomfort may dissipate simply because we are taking time to breathe and de-stress. Or, de-stressing may only occur through an external response —engaging in physical activity or taking medication. Focusing on the rhythm of our breath brings us into the moment and enhances awareness of our mental and emotional states and the steps we need to take to move into a place of calm.

Many traditions offer training in a variety of breathing techniques that intend to calm and center us mentally, emotionally, spiritually and physically. Focusing on our breath brings us into awareness of the present moment. Our breath forges and strengthens the pathway to our quiet mind. Unlike tangible tools that we may forget at home or in the office, this is one tool that we always carry with us. We are never without our breath; it will guide us to the silence in our quiet mind. Paying attention to our breath increases our awareness of the world. Our breath is life itself.

When we are upset, nervous, or afraid, our breath reflects the agitation of these emotions. Our breath provides the clue that we are caught up in these emotions rather than mindfulness. Our response flexibility is diminished. In this state we are more likely to react from the unconscious judgments and assumptions our negative emotions will trigger. The good news is that simply focusing on our breath at such times may quickly defuse a potential reaction.

Regulating our breath and returning to awareness of the present moment, we find opportunities to shift from a frenetic state of reacting into a place of serene response. By attending to our breath, we increase the chance we will respond compassionately in any circumstance. We have time to consider the best response when we relieve the pressure that is spurring us to react hurtfully.

Intent & Action: Just Breathe

One simple breathing technique involves drawing our attention to our breathing. We do not try to shift the cadence of the breath, we rest in the rhythm of our breath. As we continue to focus on the breath, we notice what happens. Our inhale naturally becomes longer and more even. When our breath shifts, so does our physical body and both our mental and emotional state. We relax. Clarity fills our quiet mind, and calms the inner tumult. The silence in our quiet mind deepens, all because we took a minute to focus on our breathing.

As we focus on our breath, we remain in the moment. We are hardly conscious of this awareness of our breath after a while. Over time, we lose the desire to live in the past or future. Through this awareness, we continually listen to within and without to find clarity. We intuitively notice when our internal monologue and resulting actions are not in alignment with our authentic self. We use our breath to discover what is affecting this alignment. Shifting the cadence of our breath invites peace into our being and clarity into our quiet mind.

Ninety-Second Release and Recovery

Ninety seconds can seem like forever when you feel the pang of a hurtful word or are afraid or filled with anger. However, this minute and a half can make all the difference to choosing to react out of the emotion or to respond compassionately. Studies have shown that the cycle of most emotions lasts approximately ninety seconds from the onset of the emotion to its last fading tinges. When we acknowledge the emotion but choose not to engage it, the emotion builds in intensity, peaks, and then dissipates in that ninety-second timeframe. Many emotions last far longer than ninety seconds when we get caught up in the emotion and feed it.

Getting caught up in the emotion and continuing to react to it is akin to riding a roller coaster. The emotion initiates, reaches it peak, then rushes down into the valley and up toward the next peak with no indication of stopping. We get used to the rush of emotion. Even our memory of the event triggering the emotion has the potential to propel us up the next peak. As long as we feed the emotion with self-righteous indignation and our fear-filled illusions, we perpetuate the emotion. All of our energy is drawn into sustaining a cycle that debilitates instead of giving life as long as we focus on the emotion. And sometimes that cycle lasts a very long time.

Recognizing our hurt and suffering is important. We learn from situations by understanding our feelings and how they were triggered. If we cannot get beyond feelings and release the angst they cause, we will never reach true understanding of who we are. However, we can move through the hurt and into our authentic self with compassion. At any time during the cycle of the emotion we can acknowledge its intensity and consider how the emotion hooks us. Once we recognize the hook, the fear or illusion we are attached to, we can remove it. No matter how painful releasing that hook is, allowing it to remain part of our identity depletes our energy, bolsters our illusion, and causes long-term suffering.

After we move through the ninety seconds, our emotion will have dissipated enough for us to clearly hear our internal monologue. If we listen to our reactions with the ear of our heart, we can regain our peace. We recognize the trigger, the assumption or judgment that stirred the emotion in the first place, and better understand how the emotion hooked us. When we are aware of the impulse to react, we do not even get on the roller coaster car. We know what is ahead, so we do not get hooked. We disengage the hook by acknowledging our hurt, anger, anxiety, fear — whatever emotion has the potential to trap us. Although we feel the emotion, we do not react to it.

We practice self-compassion during our response to the emotion instead. Interrupting the reactive cycle means practicing non-attachment and being non-judgmental and non-defensive. Applying three of the 4nons. Whatever we feel in the moment, we accept as life as it is. We do not let what happens define us. Our authentic spirit is our definer. We do not allow our negative emotion to take up permanent residence in our quiet mind and continue to disturb our silence.

As we use our breath to move through the emotion; we do not judge, do not lay blame, do not defend our right to hold tight to the emotion. We let go of any personal agenda and simply let the emotion run its ninety- second cycle. We acknowledge the emotion but do not allow our authentic self to be hooked by it. At the end of a very short roller-coaster ride, we disembark leaving the emotion behind. We move into the next moment.

Disengaging the emotion in ninety seconds is not easy. We are human, we get hurt, we suffer. It is in our nature to feel and react instinctively to pain or fear. But, this reactivity does not serve our intent to be compassionate to our self or others. Through the practice of release and recovery, we are empowered to move more quickly through the emotion and release it. Only after the emotion is gone are we able to share compassion with our self and others. As with all things, practice is most important.

Our Quiet Mind

Cultivating the silence in our quiet mind increases our awareness and our ability to be in the present moment. Clarity flourishes in the silence. With clarity we respond to life triggers non-defensively. We respond from our quiet mind instead of tumultuous confusion. Our focus is on the compassionate intent that resides in our quiet mind. Being aware of our internal monologue makes all the difference. As we listen to our internal monologue despite the turmoil and distractions, we respond.

A quiet mind is developed trough the contemplative practice of full body listening. When we bring awareness to our entire being, we are better able to hear our internal monologue. We gain a wealth of information about our authentic self, about our illusions, and about how both form our reality. We acknowledge the triggers that cause us to react and identify the harmful effects of our reactions to them. By listening to our monologue we recognize the judgments and assumptions that are at the root of many of our reactions. The quiet mind eventually opens the portal through which we hear the voices of our body, heart, mind, and spirit. These voices are our connection to the Sacred. By listening intently we sift through our illusions and find the primary resident of our quiet mind, our authentic self.

We engage our quiet mind and use the silence as a pathway to shifting our focus. During this shift of focus we notice our physical stance: where we hold our tension, where we are relaxed, and how we physically respond and react to others and to our environment. We respond to these clues in ways that relieve our suffering or discomfort.

After we attend to our suffering with compassion, we can begin to honestly identify our illusions and reframe our reality authentically. While it may take time for our quiet mind to be able to unveil what lies at the root of the illusion we are defending, each time we engage our awareness, we discover more of what underlies the illusion. With awareness we gain the courage to respond to the illusion.

We intuitively respond from our quiet mind when we are in the present moment. Although we may have thoughts based on worries and have regrets about the past, we recognize that these are illusions. They have no place in the present moment. We may be aware of these triggers, but we know we have the choice not to react to them. Instead we can respond compassionately in the present moment.

Each time we respond with our quiet mind we gain the strength not to cling or to dwell on these worrisome thoughts. Within the silence of our quiet mind, we understand that the past is what it is and cannot be changed. When angst over some past hurt surfaces, our ninety-second release and recovery strategy strengthens our silence and refocus our quiet mind. As we respond to an emotion instead of reacting to it, we engage compassion more fully in the present moment.

Focusing on the future with its worries, concerns, and fears jerks us out of the present moment, too. With a future-focus, we become passengers in a supersonic train rushing headlong down an unfinished track. Unless we can move into the present moment, a train wreck is inevitable. We cannot think about the future without activating illusions. Fantasies put our real life journey on hold and diminish self awareness in the moment. While we can and should make plans for the future, such plans are only realized by engaging our quiet mind in the present. Staying in the moment means we are able to see where we are now. We recognize the fear, angst, or worries of the present and respond to them in real time. We make the course corrections now that keep us safe by securing the path.

To grow the silence in the quiet mind, we identify what increases clarity, encourages response, and reduces reactions. As often as possible, we replicate the conditions that create this environment. Through our quiet mind, silence flows to all aspects of our life. A quiet mind is sustained and deepened through our awareness of the present moment. Through the silence of the quiet mind, responding to life's interactions is easier. We are aware of when we are non-attached, non-judgmental, non-defensive, and non-violent and when we are not.

The 4Nons

    One contemplative practice each of us can do is to rest in the silence of our quiet mind for ten minutes each day. During this time we listen to our internal monologue and notice the assumptions and judgments that we hear over and over. We gently consider whether we may have an agenda or ulterior motive. The worries, regrets, or fears that lure us from the present moment into the past or future are identified.

    To accomplish this awareness exercise we use the 4nons: non-attachment, non-judgment, non-violence, non-defensiveness. The 4nons invite us to be aware of our thoughts without owning, negating, reacting, or excusing what resides in our quiet mind. The 4nons help us to identify our authentic self and dispel any illusions. Using the 4nons encourages our authentic self to come out from behind our illusions and engage compassion.

Being Non-attached

    Non-attachment asks us to notice what we cling to and what we push away. We identify our beliefs, judgments, and motives as triggers that threaten to attach or detach us from our authentic self in a particular situation or interaction. Non-attachment is not apathy. It is a willingness to be objective and question whether our beliefs and judgments strengthen our authentic nature or not. Non-attachment is a kind of courage. We may want to cling to our illusions because they are familiar patterns of thought and action that seem to provide security. However, with courage, we can let go of what we think and discover what is really true about our self. If we are non-attached we can take that leap.

Acknowledging that we cling to certain beliefs, judgments, and desires that are illusory takes courage. When we are non-attached we can begin to identify the illusions and fears attached to them. With self-compassion we understanding our hesitancy to let go of certain illusions and remind our self to hold our hesitancy like water in the palm of our hand. We regard the illusion, we reflect on its purpose. When we understand that we do not need it, we release it. We open our self to another way, another belief, a more authentic being. Being non-attached asks that we suspend beliefs and judgments with humility. We rest in the unknown and accept ourselves for who we are. This is accomplished with courage and curious daring.

Being Non-judgmental

We all make judgments every moment of every day. Some judgments are necessary and likely to have little impact on our self or others; for example, what we plan to prepare for our evening meal. However, some judgments form the base of our biases or harmful attachments. When we make this type of judgment, we cause harm and suffering in the world. Judgments we make with self- awareness contribute to our authentic, compassionate nature.

We want to distinguish the judgments that strengthen our authentic, compassionate self from those that only mire us in unknowing and self-illusion. Right judgment empowers our compassionate intent, from which truly compassionate action flows. False judgments about our self and others constrict compassion's flow.

Being non-judgmental does not mean we never make another judgment in our life. Practicing a non-judgmental stance asks us to rest in the silence of our quiet mind and listen without attachment to our judgments. Only when we are non-attached, does our quiet mind serves as a filter for our judgments. We recognize which judgments are illusions and which are true. We accept that we are conduits of both compassion and harm. When we are non-judgmental, we choose not to react in harmful and hurtful ways; rather, we choose to respond from the ground of our being, love.

Being Non-violent

A definition of violence is necessary in order to adopt a non-violent stance. For me, violence is any word, action, or thought has the potential to harm or hurt another. Violence may be as overt as hitting someone or as subtle as having denigrating thoughts about another. When we live from our first foundational awareness, cause no harm, we are living from a non-violent stance.

Non-violence asks us to examine our judgments and assumptions to identify which are laden with either overt or subtle violence. Honesty and compassion are required as we use our non-violent filter to discover which thoughts, actions, and words are aggressive and hurtful. Being non-violent requires that we consciously re-pattern all harmful thoughts, words, and actions into ones that are gentle, loving, and compassionate. Being hyperaware is necessary to the honest recognition and shift of our violent reactions to compassionate responses.

Intent & Action: Another Look at Violence

Impatience can blossom into violent thoughts that can trigger violent actions and words. I remember being frustrated with a woman who was crossing a street very slowly in front of my car. I had to brake and wait as she crossed. I watched as she struggled across the street. Although I wanted to blow my horn, I restrained myself. But my aggravation and irritation ran amuck in my mind. My thoughts were very hurtful. Although the violence remained within me, it was violence all the same.

Several months later, when I hurt my back, I was the woman struggling to cross the street. I received hurtful comments and gestures. Then I remembered how I had reacted to the woman who had struggled to cross the road in front of me. This was an epiphany. When I was on the receiving end of others anger and frustration, I realized the violence I had perpetrated on the other woman.

This understanding has flowed into many other areas of my life. When I find myself making harsh judgments or being critical, I remind myself that there is much that I am not seeing and even more that I do not understand. Non-judgment and non-violence support each other. If we fully commit to causing no harm with our thoughts, we can become non-violent and a wellspring of compassion in our pain-filled world.

Becoming a non-violent person requires we rest in the silence of our quiet mind while paying attention to the tenor of our internal monologue. we acknowledge how our inner voice is the parent of our words and actions. Being non-violent means we are also non-judgmental and non- attached when we are interacting with others.

Some of our judgments and assumptions are laden with subtle violence. Our thoughts, actions, and words may be aggressive and hurtful. If what we are doing, thinking, or saying is not gentle, loving, or compassionate, chances are there is violence lurking within and behind our words. Being aware of the violence within our internal monologue is necessary if we want to dispel the illusion that violent thoughts do us no harm. When we acknowledge they do harm to our self and others, we begin to engage compassion with authentic intent and purposeful action.

In summary, non-violence invites us to rest in the silence of our quiet mind while paying attention to the tenor of our thoughts, words, and actions. Being non-violent requires that we are non-judgmental and non-attached to what we discover. It is never easy to accept the subtle ways that we perpetrate violence. Our goal is to acknowledge existing violence and modify any thoughts, words, or actions that are violent in nature.

Being Non-defensive

Identifying our thoughts, our assumptions, our motives, and our propensity for violence can be disconcerting and embarrassing. We might prefer to defend actions and words that expose who we really are and ignore the harm we cause. This defensive posture is always trigger by an illusion. We cannot be authentic unless we stop defending our self.

Of course letting go of our defensive behaviors may make us feel vulnerable. We might question how others will accept our true self when our human frailties are exposed. When we accept that our defenses are illusions, we let go the false mirrors that distort life and our self. By choosing not to defend our indefensible actions, we strengthen our authentic core. Even though this letting go may not be comfortable, it is a relief to com- passionately release the self-illusions that only pretend to secure and strengthen us. In this release, we meet our authentic self each time we enter the silence of our quiet mind to reflect.

When we are non-defensive, we are humble. We embrace our imperfections as graces, as gifts to be used on our life journey. We express compassion toward our self by accepting behaviors we cannot defend without making excuses. We change behaviors that cause suffering for our self and others. With each illusion revealed we see more clearly our real, authentic self. With joy and wholeness, we can engage compassion through our intent and action.

Discernment & Consensus

Discernment is a process for reflecting and coming to sufficient understanding in order to make a choice. The RI^2 process we have talked about and practiced together is used in the personal, holistic decision-making process that is discernment. We gather information by full-body listening. We tap into our internal monologue to discover what our body, mind, spirit, and heart are telling us. We also engage in full-body listening when we engage others in order to catch verbal and non-verbal clues. Many of the choices we must discern and conflicts we must resolve involve others. We must gather information from them too. As we reflect and introspect, we identify any illusions that may be obstacles to understanding, and we vow to be authentic, humble, and honest during our discernment. With curious daring and courage, we open our awareness to all possible solutions.

The silence in our quiet mind provides the environment through which we conceive and give birth to a resolution that reflects our true intent. We listen with the ear of our heart and trust others to listen as well. Without attachment or defensiveness, we share our ideas of potential resolution and listen to others' share theirs. This is a time of communal curious daring, courage, and eager anticipation as we remain unattached to our desired resolution and trust that whatever we each need will be part of our communal resolution.

Discernment begins when we set our intent to expose an issue's many facets. We seek to be objective and gain full knowledge. While our quiet mind is vital to discernment, we also engage the 4nons as we gather information and reflect on what it means to any potential outcome. Then we notice whether we are interpreting the knowledge differently than others and try to understand why and how our interpretation differs. Without judgment or defensiveness we strive to understand their perspectives.

Even though we may desire one outcome, we are non-attached and remain open to other outcomes. We do not judge, let alone diminish, the desires of others. Our words and actions are impeccable; we choose to act in ways that are neither defensive nor even subtly threatening. As we discern, we hunt for the illusions that limit our choices and accentuate our differences. Our focus remains on what will bring about the most good. This is the compassionate response we want to ensure.

Discernment is not a quick process. The time spent is well worth the result. Often, group discernment is less about deciding on an outcome than growing a community around a common good. Discernment at its best invites us to enter into communion:

to engage in a deep communication that allows us to become one in mind and heart with others.

If we are discerning with a group, we aim for consensus. Consensus differs from compromise. When reaching consensus we mediate instead of negotiate. Compromise is an intermediate solution. Both sides give and take; they meet in the middle. Consensus, on the other hand, is not content with the middle ground. Consensus is interested in finding common ground. In this place harmony and understanding reside. It is in our common ground that compassion flourishes.

When we work toward consensus, we bring a clear understanding of what we want to the discussion. We also bring a willingness to suspend our wants and enter into deep dialogue, reflection, and introspection with others. The RI^2 process can greatly facilitate group discernment. When we begin a discernment process, we may think that we clearly know what we want for the group. We need to let that particular understanding go for it is an illusion.

Our stance during consensus reaching is open, wise, and understanding. We listen with the ear of our heart to the hopes and desires of the other. We share ours without judgment and without defending our position. In the silence of our connected minds and hearts, we reach consensus and rest on common ground. We are fully engaged in communion.

This process of consensus building is not easy, nor does it provide a quick fix. It takes time, effort, humility, and courageous intent to reach consensus. We may need to return to discern the issue and then tweak the decision that we had made earlier. Both discernment and consensus are dynamic, living processes of community building. The end result of discernment is not a meeting in the middle; it is coming to a place of true harmony: our common ground.

Recollection

Recollection, taking a long loving look at the real, is a practice used in many spiritual traditions. It involves taking time, in the present moment, to reflect on life as it is and as it has been. We do not recollect to relive old hurts but to appreciate where we are now and to reaffirm our commitment to engaging compassion through intent and action: to laying the deck of our bridge.

When we regularly take a loving intentional look at the real, we develop a specific way of looking at life. In time and with practice, recollection becomes spontaneous, unconscious, and ongoing. Through recollection we may recall the negative patterns we re-routed in order to find our authentic path. Recollection is directly related to the fourth pillar supporting our foundational consciousness: Taking A Loving Intentional Look at Life. However, the practice of recollection requires engaging the other three pillars as well: Being Present, Understanding Our Self, Living with Curious Daring. It is not always comfortable to look back and reflect.

When practicing recollection, we may become conscious of some illusions that persist in our life even though we have been working to root them out through listening to our internal monologue and responding compassionately. With compassion for our self, we now look back over the life we have lived and the course corrections we have already made. We affirm ourselves for the illusions we have dispelled through our contemplative practice. We consider what additional obstacles prevent our living compassionately. To recollect, we may use the RI^2 process to ask what lingering hurts and memories are binding our feet and what prevents us from taking risks. We may search for cracks in any of the deck tiles we have laid and discern if we might replace them. We question how we have accepted life as it is.

When we practice recollection, we recall, name, and integrate those responses that accentuate what is right in our world. We acknowledge persistent illusions and creatively problem solve resolutions. Recollection helps us sustain positive life patterns and reroute the ones that may still be causing harm. We might think of recollection as slowing down to look at how we have constructed our bridge. We look outward at the patterns that form our life and are reflected in the water below. In the moment, aware of our personal reality, we notice that we are living authentically and grounded on the bridge we have built so far. We keep an eye out for illusions that are still obstacles to our fully engaging compassion.

In other words, we recall and integrate what we know to be authentic expressions of our self; we anchor our essence in our quiet mind. Through this grounded connection, we resonate closer to the real and drift farther from the thought, words, and behaviors that are signs of our illusions. By now, most are simply "water under the bridge."

As with all of our life, we start wherever we are during recollection. We accept life as it is. Recollection reminds us that life is as it should be. The intent of recollection is to strengthen the connection to our authentic self in the present moment. This connection draws us closer to understanding who we are and provides the impetus to recognize and release our illusions. Recollection reminds us to secure our foundation. Life is as it is, and we are who we are. If we feel less than secure in our foundation, we are hesitant about acting upon our intent.

RI^2: Reflection, Introspection & Integration

This process is always available to us when we need to deepen our awareness of what we are facing in the present moment and want to respond compassionately to it.

Each of the tools mentioned in this chapter are actually used during RI^2. We enter into the silence by focusing on our breath. Within that silence, we access our quiet mind and listen to our internal monologue. Perhaps we become aware that we are caught up in a reaction of some sort either fear, anger, or some persistent angst. As we begin RI^2, we remember the 4nons, which are vital to using the ninety-second release and recover strategy that helps return to silence in our quiet mind. We continue to use the 4nons to honor our authenticity and release the illusions we identified upon reflection.

We continue RI^2 with introspection, that is, the discernment of what is affecting us and why. Finally, we integrate the new understanding of our self and our circumstances. We determine how we will respond with compassion. Let us look at each stage of RI^2 more closely.

Reflection

Reflection always begins within the silence of our quiet mind. Within our inner silence we are aware of the present moment. Only within the present moment do we honestly identify what is real and authentic. We unveil our illusions when we become aware of what we are feeling at present. Then we reflect on our inner dialogue to find what thoughts are triggering an emotional reaction at present. We seek awareness in order to respond compassionately instead of reacting.

Reflection is a natural outcome of our awareness. When we notice, without judgment or defensiveness, we recognize what we are attached to. We engage our internal monologue, even if we are having a conversation with another person. We listen both externally and internally to what is stimulating our reactions and what is preventing us from responding.

When we engage in this deep awareness, we identify patterns that have been created by an illusion that we feel we have to defend. Full body listening may allow us to access our authentic self who alone can stand against the waves of illusion and make a compassionate response. Once we identify our pattern or illusion, we do not label it as good or bad. It is simply information we need next step in our RI^2 discernment: introspection.

Introspection

We use any information we glean about our self and the world from our reactions and responses. Some of this knowledge we discover by listening to our inner monologue before it is spoken or acted upon. What information we discover through our internal monologue we more fully consider in the next phase of RI^2 — introspection.

Introspection involves identifying the assumption, judgment, or fear at the root of what is triggering our reactions. Using the 4nons, we consider how the assumption or judgment we are making create the illusion from which we react. How is the assumption or judgment contributing to our misunderstanding? Through introspection we identify patterns that contribute to our reactive behavior and search for ways to turn those reactions into responses.

Using the 4nons during introspection helps us to remain authentic and not be caught in a cycle of defensive reaction. Uncovering coping mechanisms and acknowledging reactions to life triggers can be a humbling experience. We clearly see how our judgments and assumptions are at the root of our reactive behavior. Once identified, our gut instinct is to defend or justify our behavior, or we may become self-critical and depressed. If we engage the 4nons, we can move forward in ways that avoid either polar reaction.

The beginning of non-attachment is the realization that we do cling; we are attached. While we may not be ready or able to let go, expressing our desire to be open to other options may break the grip of this attachment and help us honestly enter into introspection. We engage in a life-long process of reflecting and introspecting in order to honor our authentic being and release the illusions. With practice, the process becomes easier, if not natural.

Introspection asks us to name our judgments and assumptions while examining how we are getting stuck in them. We seek to better understand our interactions with the world and gain clues to the roots of our illusions. As we practice introspection, we resist defending our judgments and assumptions and any word or action that stems from them and prompt us to be less than compassionate.

Peering deeply into the roots of our illusions, we study what triggers our reactions. Once we recognize the triggers, we can try to understand them while resting in the silence in our quiet mind. Our focus is on our triggers and our awareness is on our choice to react or respond. The better able we are to identify the triggers and transform our reactions into responses, the more we engage compassion through intent and action.

Integration

The final step in RI^2 is integration. We integrate the knowledge gained through reflection and understanding obtained through introspection. We find a common ground in which our interactions shift from reactions to responses. Integration is the result of applying knowledge and understanding in order to make right judgments. Such choices are made with authenticity, humility, and courage.

RI^2 calls us to be authentic by acknowledging our illusions and choosing to be reverent in all of our relation- ships. With reflection, introspection, and integration, we rest within the silence of our quiet mind and embrace the wonder and awe of who we are. We see without illusion that this wonder and awe is present in all of creation.

In RI^2 we use the Seven Gifts of the Spirit and all the tools we always carry with us. These tools, from focusing on our breath to the discernment process of RI^2, help us to identify illusions and open us to a more authentic way of being. Through RI^2 we receive opportunities to grow and sustain the silence in our quiet mind while repatterning our life to better represent our authentic reality.

RI²: Reflection, Introspection, & Integration

RI² is a contemplative practice that connects our body, mind, spirit, and heart in order to respond compassionately to something in our life.

First, we reflect with our heart. We identify what we feel without making any judgment about those feelings. We observe what is happening in our life and relationships that might relate to what we are feeling.

Second, we introspect using our logical mind. Again, without judgment, we attempt to understand what is truly amiss. We actively search for patterns of reaction.

Third, we integrate our understanding in ways that shift our fear-filled reactions to compassionate responses. More often than not, we change our thinking or behavior because we see that we were thinking and acting out of preconceptions about our self or others, rather than knowledge and understanding. This process, practiced regularly, transforms us. We become more true to our self, and more compassionate of others.

Use the following questions to reflect, introspect, and integrate transformation into your own life. Enter into a reflective place, where you just notice the many potential answers that reside in your quiet mind. Then engage your introspection. How do these responses fit with the reality of who you are? Which ones are authentic and which ones challenge your illusions? Next, integrate what you have learned by embracing what is real and true and letting go of the unreal and the untruthful. Let go of the illusion.

- How did the ninety-second rule help or hinder your release of an emotion?
- What was the response or the reaction of your internal monologue in your quiet mind?
- How did using the 4nons help you release anger, fear, sorrow or angst? Did you get hung up and therefore unable to engage one or more of them?

- Recall a past situation similar to this one. How were you successful in navigating the ninety-seconds? If you were not successful, what pattern is allowing you to get hooked and goading you to react?
- What would help you to successfully navigate the ninety-seconds?

Part 3

Walking Across The Bridge

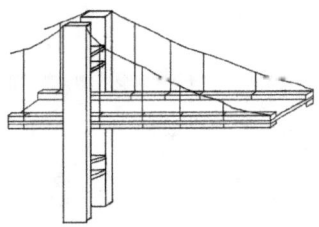

Introduction

Life is an incredible journey, a joy-filled jaunt across our life bridge. We step onto the bridge with our first inhale of air and step off the bridge on our final exhale. During this time, we lay a foundation of awareness and sink the pillars deeply into this base. We connect to our soul essence through our foundational awarenesses and live with the strategies inherent in our life pillars. We are aware of and integrate the Seven Gifts of the Spirit and choose contemplative practices that best create an environment of silence in our quiet mind. Through our quiet mind, we form our intent and engage our compassionate nature. We build our compassion bridge's deck by integrating contemplative tools into our responses.

We live our life with curious daring and authenticity; our eyes open to our life rhythms and patterns. No longer are we able to live in tedious routines that are not life giving. We are nudged sometimes with a whisper and at other times with a shout to develop new habits that enable us to take each step with a joy-filled, compassionate lightness of being. Clearly recognizing and choosing to integrate life patterns that sustain our compassionate nature, we live with authentic integrity.

Our eyes open to the possibilities of transformation as we walk across the bridge. The potential for transformation happens each time we lay a deck plank. Through a better understanding of our self, we choose which practices and which tools to engage in the present moment. When we listen with the ear of our heart, our inner knowing, reveals which tool or practice places us more firmly in the moment. We manifest our intent. It propels us from span to span. With each compassionate act, the deck tiles reflect our humble, authentic spirit. We live within a never-ending cycle of learning, growth, challenge, and transformation by engaging our compassion through intent and action.

As we deepen our awareness of who we are, we release our illusions. Our authentic being surfaces. We are filled with joy, compassion, and unconditional love. This incredible journey is not meant to be a solitary one; our joy, compassion, and love are meant to be shared. Our soul overflows; it can hardly contain the effervescence of our being. We have to share; we have to be compassionate. Refusal to be compassionate casts us into a world rife with illusions.

Our desire to be a compassionate partner in community is as instinctual as breathing. We invite others to share this journey with us. Our compassion-filled life manifests through each connection and is strengthened through relationship. We share this recognized wonder and awe with others, the Sacred, and all of creation. Through this sharing, we discover a deep intimacy that is greater and more encompassing than anything we have experienced previously.

We begin to live in communion; intimacy is shared. Our friends, family, coworkers, and strangers benefit from our compassionate nature. Intimacy deepens each time we interact with unconditional love and compassion. Compassion is not a privilege or a gift or even a reward. Compassion is a right and a responsibility. As a member of the global community it is our responsibility and privilege to share compassion and our right to receive it.

Compassion begins first with our self. Next we share compassion with others and all of creation. We accept their compassion. Through this cycle of sharing and receiving, we develop an intimate connection with all whom we meet. Sharing compassion is the single most transformative act that we, as individuals and as community, can make. As each act of compassion cascades into the next, the world is radically changed, one compassion-filled act as a time.

Only through our connection with others is our view of the world challenged. Through intentional dialogue and by listening with the ear of our heart, we gain the knowledge we need to challenge our assumptions, judgments, and beliefs. As we take a long, loving look at our reality, we see the nuances filled with hidden meanings that bring us to one realization. We are not alone. We live in community no matter how alienated or alone we may feel. With others' assistance, we meet the challenge to align our reality with the truths we perceive in the world.

The affects of our words and actions on our self, others, and all of creation become apparent. When we move from a place of closed hurting to wide openness, we trigger a radical paradigm shift. We share our awareness and our compassionate actions with everyone we meet on this remarkable journey. We cast aside the heavy cloak of illusion and stand clothed in our authenticity as we share compassion.

Living intentionally and embracing the foundational consciousness of causing no harm, alleviating suffering and accepting life as it is, provides the means to shift into compassionate connection. Even amidst the suffering, we recognize our connection to others. We understand the profound effect our compassionate action has on others. We know that unless we practice our foundational awarenesses each moment, the potential exists for us to become a force for great hurt instead of compassion. By consciously accepting our role in sharing compassion, we transform our life. With our transformation, we trigger the transformation of others. We become the change we want to see in the world.

Chapter 7

Transforming Our Personal Reality

Two people engage in a conversation. Two people listen to the same lecture. Two people study the same set of facts. Ask each of those people what they heard and what conclusions they drew; each would have different understandings of the same situation. Every person has a unique set of filters and ways of perceiving the world. Each of us has our own personal reality based upon our assumption and beliefs.

We create this reality based upon what our life filters catch. Certain information hooks us, and we form our beliefs and our life views based upon the judgments and assumptions made about this information. Over time we become predisposed to gathering information that strengthens our perceptions and validates our judgments. We may unconsciously ignore information that challenges our perceived reality. We create a limited view of life as it is, and our view may be a harsh illusion. With curious daring and a long intentional look at this reality, we can remove the planks of illusion and rebuild an authentic deck.

Our personal reality is created from our many perceptions. Our understanding is based upon both awareness and lack of awareness. With our assumptions, judgments, motives, and agendas, we draw conclusions and accept beliefs. We are unaware of the false ground on which they lay.

If we blindly accept our judgments, our illusion-filled reality is strengthened. The view is further reinforced through our reactions to life triggers and to the reactions of others. While a viewpoint is never "wrong" per se, it might be filled with illusions built upon the inaccuracies and fallacies that our judgments and assumptions have spawned. Challenging our views non-defensively and with curious daring provides the only way for us to move into a more authentic reality.

We are born tabula rasa, a clean slate. At birth we have no preconceived notions or predetermined judgments and assumptions. Our senses are wide open, and we indiscriminately consume all information we receive. We are unable to process all the information bombarding us. In the beginning, we have no filters or boundaries. Survival is our only motivation. We lack experience and must rely on our instincts. While we are open to all stimuli and sensations in the world, we react to those that startle us or make us feel uncomfortable or hungry. We learn how to get attention, so we are soothed and calmed, will get our diaper changed, or receive nourishment. Early we discover which trigger gets reactions and which stimulates responses. We create an intuitive understanding of our self and others by experiencing all of these reactions and responses. Thus begins the creation of our reality. From our first inhale, we process information and do not stop processing until the final exhale.

As we grow in awareness and form connections to others, the first relationships we form are with our parents and our primary caregivers. Next we form additional relationships with family, friends, and other members of community. Each relationship impacts our view of the world. Consciously and unconsciously, we absorb information and act upon both verbal and non-verbal cues from the world around us. The judgments, motives, and assumptions of others affect our judgments. Our interactions are mutual; we help others to form their judgments and assumptions. If we were colicky as a baby, our mother's younger sister may have decided to postpone having a child. If someone holds us stiffly as a baby, we may not want to be held as an adult. Of course, such snap judgments are subjective and based upon a single event, rather than understanding the complexity of reason behind our reactions. Still the judgment may persist without any basis or relevance to the present.

When we enter into relationships, our personal reality intertwines with the realities of those with who we are in relationship. These two realities further twine into the collective reality of the community in which we live creating a living, organic braid of communal reality. Even if we are unaware of the impact of the personal realities of others and the communal reality, we are still impacted by the words and actions of those around us. Through our connections to others we engage and learn. We use full body listening to process the words and actions of others. Our physical body, our mind, our heart, and our spirit absorb this information. Our view of reality is furthered developed.

While facts themselves may be objective, we inevitably assign subjective meanings to them. We may react strongly to even the most objective information when it is filtered through our emotional, mental, physical, and spiritual bodies. Our feelings, emotions, and prior experiences determine how we process the information and arrive at our perceived truths. RI^2 helps us determine the truth or fallacy of our perceptions. As we begin to reflect and introspect upon these perceived truths, we identify the roots of our illusions and the depth of our authentic being.

Through our relationships, we form and sustain our reality. Each interaction encourages questioning of our beliefs or acceptance of our reality. It is through the four relationships — with our self, the Sacred, others, and all of creation — that the light shines into the window of our true authentic self.

Of course, any path to a truer reality is fraught with obstacles. When we love and trust others, we listen to them in a particular way and are more easily accepting of what we hear. If we have preconceived notions and beliefs about another person whom we do not trust, we may automatically negate their views. We hear things differently depending upon the relationship. We may ignore the cautions and questions in our quiet mind. Our old patterns are maintained and illusions accepted.

Our interactions with others whom we do not trust, respect, or even like, present a phenomenal opportunity. Within our mistrust, hurt, and wariness is the possibility of understanding. We engage the RI^2 process first by reflecting. In the present moment, we engage full body listening in order to discover what is being triggered by our interactions. Our reflection is both on what the other said and our reaction or response to it. Listening on two levels, or bi-listening, is important; we are aware of our external dialogue and our internal monologue simultaneously. We recognize that even if what others share is authentic and real, we may brand it an illusion because we do not trust or like the person who is sharing.

Using the knowledge gained we move into introspection. During this step we gain a greater understanding of why and how what happened triggered our defenses. We relax our defenses. We recognize and own our barriers to an honest listening. Through introspection we may even gain new skills to use during later interactions.

Finally we integrate what we have learned through reflection and introspection. Although our trust level with the other person may not have improved, we honestly listen to the other with an awareness of our barriers. We listen for what is said. We move past the illusion of not trusting and move into the potential for transformation of our reality and of the relationship.

Our relationships are the best windows through which we discover what is authentic and what is illusory. When we engage another in the present moment, we clearly hear our internal monologue. We identify the roots of our assumptions and judgments. A willingness to be objective is a component of listening with the ear of our heart. When we enter into relationship with love, trust, and objectivity we are more likely to identify what is authentic and what is illusory. Through this objective engagement, our reality becomes more authentic. Objective engagement is only possible by living out of the 4nons.

Relationships are not easy. Being objective may feel impossible at times. If we are unaware of our assumptions and judgments triggered by the other person, we may react to what we name as hurtful or inconsiderate or inaccurate. In these moments, we do not question our behaviors; we view them as being authentic and justified. The opposite may be true. When we care deeply for another, we trust what they say without questioning or engaging any of our filters. We may incorporate inaccuracies and illusions into our reality solely due to our relationship with the other. When we accept information in either of these ways, we sustain our illusion-filled reality.

No matter how invested we are in a relationship when we live from our four pillars, we cannot blindly accept illusions. If we rest in the silence of our quiet mind and focus our awareness in the present moment, we attend to what is occurring. The intentional look, when accomplished with curious daring, reveals our barriers as well as ways to navigate past these barriers. We understand the foundation of our responses and reactions. The intentional look necessitates an attitude of wide openness. We live from the four pillars and identify what is life-giving and what prevents us from living life fully.

Engaged compassion begins with the courage to be our self, that is, with compassion for our true self. It is not always comfortable or comforting to enter the silence of our quiet mind and listen to the internal monologue. We might be distressed or embarrassed or discouraged by what we hear. When we are present in the moment, we are aware of how our internal monologue shapes our external dialogue. We hear how we either cause harm or share compassion. The ear of our heart listens on the frequencies of both conversations. When we are intent upon living an authentic reality, we discern what is real and what is illusion. Through our discernment, we are honest about the effects of our words and actions. With this awareness, we name what is authentic and what is illusion. This identification is the first step to growing more authentic reality.

As we grow in our ability to identify what is illusory and what is authentic, we realize that the line between our authentic self and our illusory self is often blurry. It is in this foggy area that we look for and find our assumptions and judgments and discern where truth resides. If we are not living in the moment, we may miss clues that reveal skewed perceptions and underlying illusions. Within this uncertainty we discern what is real and what is false. Through understanding we create a more real, valid, and authentic reality.

No matter how inaccurate or illusory our perceptions may be, unless we can learn to recognize illusion, we will be unable to see the truth of who we are. That truth is always wondrous and freeing when we exercise compassion. As long as we are not aware of our own judgments and biases, our reality will not be authentic. It will be mired in illusion. We join hands with curious daring and courage as we enter the messy fogginess. Our intent is not to be right at all costs; rather, our intent is to find the right stuff, the building materials, with which to create and sustain the deck of our life bridge, our authentic reality.

Being present in the moment is the foundation on which we create an authentic reality. Through awareness in the moment we recognize when illusion encroaches upon our reality. Removal of the illusion happens in the present moment when we rest in the silence of our quiet mind. Although we recognize the tumult from which our angst, worry, and fear emanate, we are suffused with peace and courage. Calling upon our courage, we navigate this tumult with the clarity. Through an actively engaged quiet mind, we identify what is true and what is illusory. We then take steps to release the illusions.

We listen with the whole of our being intent on discovering the illusion surrounded by fog. As illusion is revealed, we have a choice to remain hooked by the illusion or to question it. When we discover which of our assumptions and judgments created this false sense of reality, we remove the illusion at its root. Removing it at this level is the only way to banish it from our reality. Even after uprooting the illusion, we take care to not replant its seed.

When we are awake, aware, and living in the moment, it is easier to separate what is real from our judgments and assumptions. With our eyes and ears wide open we view each interaction and listen to each conversation both separately and as a part of our entire reality. We look for patterns as we listen to how the words and ideas are connected. Adjectives hold descriptive clues to a person's judgments and assumptions. The cadence of the conversation or stress placed upon individual words or phrases shed light on the meaning behind the words. By paying attention to the other person and engaging in full- body listening, we perceive all aspects of the information and recognize how our reality is swayed by our interaction with another.

An authentic, valid reality evolves from our awareness of the external world and our understanding of our connections to it. Awareness of our responses and reactions to the actions and words of others is the precursor to understanding our own assumptions and judgments. We listen to our internal monologue and begin to discern if our assumptions and judgments are false or accurate. Based upon our conclusions we may need to reframe or refine our beliefs. Engaging in this assessment strengthens our authentic self.

Not all of our judgments are based on illusion. Some of our judgments are vital to creating and sustaining our authentic self. Some judgments keep our personal boundaries intact. For example, when I volunteer, I have to be careful not to say "yes" to every task. My agreement to do something is often based upon the relationship I have with the person making the request. My judgment to help or not is not harmful or hurtful. I make judgments not based upon whether of person is deserving of my help; rather, I ensure that I am not over-extended and maintain appropriate personal boundaries.

If a judgment is not hurtful or harmful to our self or another, it is probably one that contributes to our authentic reality. When we question the root of the judgment, we enter into the silence of our quiet mind to discover the answer. Only there can we listen to our internal monologue and are objective. Objectivity is necessary in the ongoing evaluation of what contributes to our truth and what creates the flaws in our authentic design.

These flaws or illusions are not to be arbitrarily discarded without reflection or introspection. Learning from them provides opportunities for our growth and transformation. They provide clues that show us the roots of potentially dysfunctional life patterns and reveal how we tend to nourish such patterns. When we own our judgments and assumptions, we begin the process of shifting the perception of our reality. Within this newly formed reality we become stronger, more authentic vessels of compassion.

RI^2 is a handy tool to incorporate into our daily informal contemplative practice. Using reflection and introspection we test the validity of our personal reality. We recognize our judgments through reflection and search for their roots during introspection. Introspection provides the study and analysis of our judgments' positive and negative impacts on our reality. As we integrate our findings, we release illusions and align with a more authentic reality. RI^2 is a tool through which we objectively make changes to align our reality with our truth.

This realignment occurs through an awareness of our patterns. The illusions of some patterns are obvious; others are very subtle. When we understand how we use the illusions, we can create more authentic patterns of coping. Other patterns may only appear to be illusory; but actually they are authentic to our reality. Through reflection and introspection, we discover the truth of what we really believe.

There is no harm in evaluating all of our life patterns. This is a practice in self-compassion. We may be surprised what we discover is authentic and what is illusion. Reflection and introspection are never wasted activities. They provide avenues through which we grow our authentic being. An authentic being is one who engages compassion through intent and action.

Some of our life patterns are necessary for us to function in the world. Those patterns align us to a compassion-filled life. Patterns that trigger honesty, truth, sharing, and holistic life choices are patterns that create and nourish. It is only a matter of discerning whether the patterns are also compassionate. Some patterns may appear healthy, but they actually feed our fears and intensify the illusions in our life. One illusion might be the belief that if I do "good works," I am a "good person" even if these acts cause us harm. This illusion might reflect a lack of self-compassion. Self worth is not based on what we do or do not do.

Other patterns may serve to root us in self-righteous, judgmental rationales. With daring curiosity, question all your life patterns. When you are courageously non- attached to how you live your life, you will more easily release what is not working and engage with eager anticipation what is.

We ask ourselves what is our truth and how we arrived at the place of truth. Look deeply for judgments and assumptions that are hidden in false truths or masquerading as accurate knowledge. Universal statements about "them" or the others provide big clues that we have journeyed over the fence that separates the land of objectivity from the glorious field of subjectivity. This field is awash with our illusions. When we choose to be objective, we retain our non-attached stance and remain alert for illusion.

Our reality is ours and probably, for the most part, is an accurate portrayal of our world. As we nurture the silence in our quiet mind, become more authentic, and question the foundation of our reality, we become aware of illusions and become curious about what lies behind them — what we do not yet see. Through such cracks, we peer into an alternate reality and discover a rich vein of truths that add vibrancy to our reality. No longer filtered through illusion, we see a reality based upon compassion and unconditional love. We access this truer alternate reality through courage and humility and by realizing the only thing we have to lose by embracing this reality is illusion.

The journey to an objective, illusion-free personal reality is not easy or even possible. While on the path we will always be confronted by illusion. This is our never- ending journey. Traveling this path requires a courageous heart and a commitment to being authentic. This journey involves regular self-examination, commitment to transformation, and deep humility.

When we step outside of our own agendas and acknowledge our motives and judgments, we can see with the eyes of our heart and live from our authentic center. Getting to this authentic place is sometimes a scary endeavor, but it is exhilarating, too. Navigating the path means giving up what we feel we need and want, and accepting what life is giving us. Curious daring impels us along the path of compassionate response.

By fostering a non-attached view of our reality, we accept the illusory components while understanding we must take steps to align our self with a compassionate life. We hold our reality as we would hold water in the palm of our hand, that is lightly and gently, trusting the illusion will separate from our authentic being. Through RI^2 we re-evaluate our personal reality and make compassionate action our lifelong commitment.

Peeling back the layers of our reality and confronting the judgments and assumptions that underlie our illusions can be disappointing and despair filling. Our judgments and assumptions are not without benefit. In some ways, they provide a safety net for us. They provide continuity as we move from past to present to future. Our judgments and assumption play an important role in our life. They are the basis of our life lessons. We take this journey of creating our reality step-by-step, challenge by challenge fully aware in the moment. We are awake to what the lessons teach us. We let go of our assumptions and judgments only when we have learned from them. By releasing what no longer serves us, we transform.

We cannot connect with our authentic reality without being courageously vulnerable. Vulnerability is the willingness to expose our truths without shame or fear. We accept life as it is while being aware of the risk of not being accepted by others. Even in this uncertainty, we share parts of our self with which we are not comfortable. Being authentic means having the humility to share our self, without excuses, and without defending who we are. As we live in our truth, our reality shifts and comes to reflect our authentic being. Our relationships shift too.

Taking an intentional look at our life and living from what we discover requires awareness, integrity, and honesty. With awareness, we shift from reactivity to response. The response flexibility is active each time we choose to respond instead of react as well as when we begin a reaction and shift the reaction to a response. It is through this recognition and subsequent action that we shift our reactions into responses. This shift creates an increasingly more authentic personal reality.

We respond to the world and create our personal reality in two different ways: fear-filled reaction or intuitive response. A fear-filled reaction is generated by our perceived need to protect our self. We react defensively; and, at times, our reaction may even be violent. A fear-filled reaction is the result of believing that the only important relationship is with our self. We protect our self without any consideration given to any of our other relationships.

Our reacting to the reactions of others stimulates a downward spiral of negativity. We can break this harmful cycle at any time when we respond with non-attachment and choose not to react defensively to the thoughts or actions of another. Life is what it is. We can choose to react in harmful, hurtful ways or our response can be compassion- filled. A response says we are comfortable with our true self: that our focus is on what is good and true in the world not only on what we think is in our own best interest. Through our responses, we live out of our authentic reality using our compassionate intent and action. We are compassionate to our true self as we are compassionate to others.

The alternative to fear-filled reaction is an intuitive response. Such a response is courageous, fueled by curious daring, and birthed from our authentic being. Our responses tend to be gentle, loving, and compassionate even when addressing a tough situation. We maintain a non-defended, non-violent stance even when we are responding to difficult situations. We respond with non-attachment by not taking the hurtful words or harmful actions of another personally. An intuitive response does not judge a person or the situation. We own how our thoughts, actions, and words contribute to the reactions of others. We are mindfully aware of what we think, say, and do. Our intent is that each response be full of love and compassion. Our belief is in the good of those with whom we are in relationship.

Our personal reality is not static. It organically shifts as we interact with our self and others. Illusions may briefly appear and then disappear. Our everyday life and the interactions within it form our reality moment by moment. Our past actions, judgments, and assumptions play a large role in the formation of our current reality. When we live mindfully aware of both our internal monologue and our external dialogue, we more easily identify the truth and the illusion in our personal reality. We question with courage and daring all of our judgments and assumptions. We strengthen our reality and take steps to banish illusion and rest in an authentic reality.

When we recognize the illusions, we trace our life patterns back to their roots and then forward to the present moment. Through reflection and introspection, we discern if they are in alignment with our authentic self or if they are in discord. Through integrity, courage, and humility, we synchronize with those life-giving patterns and create a personal reality that better mirrors our authentic self. Our desire to be our authentic self without excuses or justifications becomes reality. We are authentic because it is the only choice we can make when living a compassion filled life.

RI²: Reflection, Introspection, & Integration

RI² is a contemplative practice that connects our body, mind, spirit, and heart in order to respond compassionately to something in our life.

First, we reflect with our heart. We identify what we feel without making any judgment about those feelings. We observe what is happening in our life and relationships that might relate to what we are feeling.

Second, we introspect using our logical mind. Again, without judgment, we attempt to understand what is truly amiss. We actively search for patterns of reaction.

Third, we integrate our understanding in ways that shift our fear-filled reactions to compassionate responses. More often than not, we change our thinking or behavior because we see that we were thinking and acting out of preconceptions about our self or others, rather than knowledge and understanding. This process, practiced regularly, transforms us. We become more true to our self, and more compassionate of others.

Use the following questions to reflect, introspect, and integrate transformation into your own life. Enter into a reflective place, where you just notice the many potential answers that reside in your quiet mind. Then engage your introspection. How do these responses fit with the reality of who you are? Which ones are authentic and which ones challenge your illusions? Next, integrate what you have learned by embracing what is real and true and letting go of the unreal and the untruthful. Let go of the illusion.

In one sense we paint our personal reality, as we build our bridge, from what we learn about our authentic self through reflecting, introspecting, and integrating what we learn to understand. The following questions are about the personal reality we have painted.

- What is your personal reality? Who are you? Look with curious daring and picture who rests in the deepest, most interior place of your being.
- How are you sharing this vulnerable self?
- How are you coating yourself with illusion? Consider judgments you make about yourself and others? Are they valid? Which judgments are suspicious?
- How is your view of reality encouraging or inhibiting intimacy?
- What is your communication style?
- Name as many moments as you can in which you know you entered into communion with your self and another.
- How do you share compassion with yourself?
- Create a montage that represents the elements within your personal reality.

Chapter 8

Start Where You Are: Walking in Compassionate Connection

We live every moment of our life connected to the world around us. By being mindful we nurture the silence in our quiet mind and compassionately respond to our self, others, the Sacred, and all of creation. We connect with our self by listening and responding to the whispers of our internal monologue. We connect to the Sacred through the silence in our quiet mind. Our compassionate action and response to our self strengthens our connections to others.

We connect with all of creation through our actions. Any contact we have with any part of creation forms a relationship. Each of these contacts, no matter how brief, becomes one of the strands of our relationship braid. Each compassionate act strengthens the weave and connects us more fully to all relationships.

Our first action upon entering this world is to inhale our last act is to exhale. Everything in between — each breath, each action, each thought, and each word – are reminders that we exist in relationship to all of creation. We choose how we are in relationship. We can intentionally engage others compassionately or we can sully our connections with hurtful actions. Most of us run the gamut from causing harm to trying to alleviate suffering. It is often difficult to discern how to respond to a situation. We are not always intentional in our reactions. As we live with foundational awareness, this balancing act of causing harm and sharing compassion shifts. We set our intent to become more compassionate and less hurtful. Over time, this intent directs us to respond ever more compassionately.

Being Present and Understanding Who We Are, the first two pillars, help us to define who we are in authentic, compassionate ways. We cannot change the hurtful reactions of the past, but through one compassionate act at a time, we positively impact our present moment. With our responses we reroute the hurt and harm producing patterns that caught us off balance in the past. We become a person filled with compassionate intent.

Contemplative living requires that we enter into our core relationships in ways that bring us into communion. Communion, the deepest form of communication, invites us to go beyond a superficial connection of words and enter deeply into connection and solidarity. In communion, we are aware of the common good that binds us to another: love.

Although we may sometimes feel disengaged from others and the world, this separation is only an illusion. At no time in our life are we not connected. We connect to others by the invisible threads formed by our thoughts, actions, and words. We twist and fray those threads with our hurtful reactions; we strengthen them with compassionate intent and action. In each moment, we build our bridge.

The stability of our compassion bridge and the beauty of its deck depend upon our life choices — choosing to be hurtful or to be compassionate. We are never alone on our bridge. We walk the deck of our bridge in relationship. We walk the decks of others' bridges that intersect with ours when we form relationships. We create our reality through the interconnections created by our relationships.

We build our bridge and live our life while in relationship. Our life is filled with intimate connections, and we realize that being alone and separate is an illusion. Intimacy forms when we connect with the other person in ways that are wordless and compassion filled. This connection of intimacy reverberates within the heart, the body, the mind, and the spirit. This resonance creates communion, and we align with the others in loving, gentle ways. The potential for this deep, wordless connection occurs each time we share unconditional love and compassion.

In deep, long-term relationships intimacy is easily recognized and identified. We are in sync; we always understand the other. We may finish their sentences or communicate with the eyes and ears of our heart. A touch, look, or our simple presence conveys love, compassion, and solidarity. Being in this kind of relationship is comfortable.

Our relationship with the Sacred and our self is forged through such an intimate connection. This intimacy is more difficult to describe, in part, because we seldom think about intimacy with our self or the Sacred. When we live out of our authentic self and listen to and respond from our internal monologue, we are engaging in intimacy. This profound connection is strengthened during reflection and introspection. Each time we let go of an illusion, we deepen our authentic connection to our own essence, our authentic self. Through this intimacy we connect to the Sacred in profound ways that may be difficult to even recognize or accept.

Our intimacy with another deepens when we acknowledge their divine spark. We become vulnerable and open to hurt when we are intimate with another. When we couple intimacy with courage, we reap the benefits of love and compassion. This is true when we engage a stranger intimately. I had not expected to share intimacy with a stranger opening a door for me at Starbucks; yet, unexpectedly, I did. We connected with our hearts and spirits when our eyes met, and I thanked him. I felt his respect for me; and in this moment of intimacy, our mutual respect morphed into reverence.

On another occasion, a hurtful situation morphed into an intimate compassion filled one. While at the grocery store, a woman in front of me in the checkout was extremely slow taking her items from her cart. I felt my irritation build until it was rolling off of me. I was not physically harming her although she may have felt my frustration with her. She turned to me and struck up a conversation mentioning that she had constant pain in her back. It was as if she apologized for holding me up. My feelings of aggravation and irritation shifted. I responded compassionately in the next moment. I wished her well. An intimacy was shared, despite my hurtful thoughts. We connected through compassionate response.

Although there are many self-help tools guaranteed to improve relationships and deepen intimacy, self-awareness is the primary tool. Through self-awareness we understand how we live out of our internal monologue. We recognize that how we respond or react to others has a lasting impact. It sets the tone for relationships no matter how brief they may be.

We foster self-awareness through our intent to share compassion and in our compassionate acts. Aware- ness expands the silence in our quiet mind. As we nurture this silence, opportunities to share compassion are revealed. Each time we respond to the compassionate nudge, intimacy in our relationships deepens. Our intuition becomes the guide to entering communion and deep intimacy. We remain in communion when we are in the present moment and engage in full body listening. To fully understand communion, it must be experienced in ways that are timeless, wordless, and profoundly intimate. Communion only occurs when we are fully aware and fully awake in the present moment.

Entering into communion with another occurs when we engage in full body listening, and we mindfully attend to the effects of our internal monologue on our intuitive responses and fear-filled reactions. It takes practice to recognize how the other person wants to be in relationship with us as well as determining how we want to be in relationship with them. We discover these answers through both verbal and non-verbal cues. We use these cues to develop intimacy in the relationship. Of course, we can reflect on these questions and discern the answers by using RI^2. After reflecting on what we know about our self and the other person, we introspect and we discern both our ability to be what the person needs and whether the other person in the relationship is capable of meeting our needs. We use this new understanding to make compassionate choices concerning our relationships.

Start Where You Are: Walking in Compassionate Connection

Being in relationship invites us into intense self-discovery through engaged intimacy and communion. Within the mirror of our relationship, we discover both our authentic being and our illusions. We practice curious daring in our relationships by entering the doorway of communion. When in communion, we courageously articulate our ability to be in relationship in loving, gentle, non-harmful, non-hurtful ways. In this journey to gain and keep intimacy, the road to authentic relationships is not illusion-free, pain free, or even comfortable. Communion is the reward that comes through honest and authentic efforts to build intimacy.

At the foundation of our ability to connect with others is our relationship with our self. We cannot enter into balanced relationships with others unless we have a loving, grounded relationship with our authentic self. This connection is created with courage, compassion, and humility. If we cannot love our self unconditionally and show compassion to our self, we cannot share love and compassion with others. This is the underlying truth of the quest to be a person of compassion.

Our relationship with our self is not created in a vacuum. If we waited until we were in authentic relation- ship with our self to enter a relationship with another, we would never have another relationship. In this incredible journey, others help us learn; they stretch us, and they lovingly invite us to be authentically who we are. We offer them a safe place to do the same. Intimacy is deepened when we take chances.

When we are authentic, we courageously and honestly accept who we are and recognize the false face our illusions create. Humbly, we recognize our limitations and our motivations. We understand how our judgments and assumptions impact our interactions with others. We match our illusions with the assumptions and judgments at their roots. Accepting who we are, we take strides to rid our self of our illusions. With each illusion we release, we move into greater alignment with our authentic self. Our words and actions represent our authentic thoughts and beliefs. Through these actions, we sustain our authentic self and enter into real and honest relationships.

With the gift of humility, we shed illusions and strip ourselves of fear-filled reactions, arrogant behavior, and pride-filled beliefs. There is no room for pride or arrogance or self-importance in any relationship. Humility asks us to be respectful, non-defensive and non-violent toward our self and others. Our actions become the gateway through which we intentionally live a compassionate life.

No longer defensive, we are able to challenge our attitudes, assumptions, and judgments in non-attached ways. Our humility offers us no room for hurtful judgment, clinging attachment, and defensive behavior. In fact, humility invites us to share compassion as a balm for our suffering. We acknowledge our imperfections, fallibilities, and humanness. By embracing what is true, we release the illusions and move into alignment with our authentic spirit.

Authenticity and humility opens the portal to our radical transformation. When these are paired with daring curiosity, we cross the threshold and explore our life with wonder and awe. The parts of us that are judgmental, violent, attached, and defensive are released, and we re-pattern our life so that only compassion and unconditional love remain. With our desire to be authentic and our courage, we power this transformation.

Being authentic aligns our self with compassion's true nature. With compassion we connect on loving, gentle, intimate levels. We are in communion built upon the connective framework of relationships. Upon this framework, we lay the deck of our bridge. Our intent begins in the silence of our quiet mind and manifests through communion in relationships. Intent and communion impel us into compassionate action.

Inner silence is not a cessation of noise; rather, this silence occurs when our minds are quiet and hyperaware. This awareness is multi-dimensional. When we dialogue with another, we are aware of how the external dialogue meshes or clashes with our internal, personal monologue. Through mindful awareness, we identify which thoughts, actions, or words are harmful or hurtful. We shift from a fear-filled reaction to an intuitive response. This response is the sharing of compassion through communion.

Start Where You Are: Walking in Compassionate Connection

When our quiet is in alignment with our authentic spirit, our responsible flexibility is pliable. In a heartbeat we recognize our trigger, our potential reaction, and our choice. We can react using old patterns, or we can create new patterns of response. With the voice of our authentic self we loudly proclaim our choice of response. Within the quiet mind, we not only recognize the possibilities to be authentic, but we also are able to process our choices rapidly. Our body, mind, spirit, and heart enter into communion with our authentic self, time expands, we respond with compassion. It is within the silence that we find intimacy with the Sacred.

In the Bible (Kings 19: 11-13), Elijah heard the great powerful wind, felt the explosion of rock, was tumbled by an earthquake, and felt the heat of the fire. He chose not to react to those false triggers. None of those events were from the Sacred. Resting within the silence of the quiet mind, he recognized the Sacred not in the helter-skelter of fright, but in a gentle whisper of the breeze. He responded to that still, small voice. He knew it was authentic, and he entered into communion. We can choose to be in the silence, like Elijah, and wait patiently until we hear the cues that call forth a loving, compassionate, authentic response, or we can continue riding a roller coaster of reacting to whatever happens.

Communion through silence and the quiet mind cannot be attained overnight. A quiet mind is cultivated in awareness of the moment. Practice, practice, and more practice combined with hyper-awareness enhances and expands the silence of our quiet mind until even the greatest angst or anger will only stimulate a tiny ripple on its surface. Our response flexibility increases the awareness that our only true option is a loving, gentle response. When this recognition occurs, we are truly living in intimate relationship.

Engaging compassion occurs through intent and action. Intent is nurtured in the silence of our quiet mind. We intend to be a font of unconditional love and dedicate our life to keeping our hearts and minds open by sharing only love with the others. Our vow is to cause no harm. Harm is impossible to cause when we are in communion with others. Through our intent and being in communion with others and the Sacred, compassionate action is continually birthed.

Through our internal monologue and with compassionate action, we alleviate suffering within our self and others whose lives we touch. Each relationship provides opportunities to enter into communion and alleviate suffering. Compassion is always a true, intuitive response. Its roots are found deep within the silence of our quiet mind. This compassion flows first to our self and wraps us in the unconditional love of understanding.

Deep within the silence of each of our quiet minds rests a divine spark. These sparks are like stars in a giant constellation of community. Our divine spark is not just a two-way circuit between our self and the Sacred; rather, it is part of an infinite circuit of sparks of compassion. Each time we share and receive compassion, our sparks are energized, and compassion's light and warmth grows.

Of course, sharing compassion takes courage. It is often easier and simpler to ignore the suffering of others. We may fear how a stranger or an acquaintance may respond to our compassionate act. That is when we remember our spark. When we connect our divine spark to the divine spark of another, we no longer fear the potential result of sharing compassion. The high beam intensity of divine spark-shared compassion invites us to live intentionally, authentically, and courageously. Compassion is truly our only option if we choose to live in relationship.

Understanding that we have the potential to relieve suffering means we do not judge the suffering of another or the path that led to that suffering. We share compassion without judgment while understanding that compassion is not the same as a solution to a problem. Compassion seeks to alleviate suffering while in solidarity with the other. We may lighten the load of the suffering, but we may not be able to change the situation that stimulated the suffering.

Compassion does not always give the other what he or she wants. Being compassionate is standing in solidarity with another while allowing him or her to experience the pain of life lessons and life challenges. Sharing compassion provides strength and support but may not lessen the perceived or real burden or pain of the other. While we can support another, we cannot change the fundamental root of his or her suffering. Only the other person can make those transformational changes in his or her own life. A compassionate action shines the light on our illusions and offers the path to greater authenticity of both the individual and the relationship.

While sharing compassion, we recognize our limitations. We learn the difference between being compassionate, beingco-dependent, and taking on the suffering of others. Compassion does not or should not trigger suffering in our self. We share unconditional love and support in ways that do not debilitate us. Our first and, at times, most compassionate act is to our self. Our self-compassion is the basis of our interdependent relationships.

Compassion is loving generosity. It fills us with the joy of being. If your compassion is angst producing or painful, then it is not a holistic, authentic, or reverent compassion. While there might be sorrowful feelings about the plight of the other, we do not take on another's suffering when we share compassion.

We are spirituality wired to share compassion and alleviate the suffering of others. Compassion is an intuitive reflex. We get so busy and pulled into the happenings of our day, we find it hard to live in the present moment. We ignore or do not recognize opportunities to be compassionate. When we focus on the moment and practice hyperawareness, we identify opportunities to share compassion and to accept compassion from others. This intentional being-in-the-moment increases an authentic awareness of our self and disengages our illusions. Within this framework of knowing, we can look lovingly at life as it is and share compassion with everyone we encounter.

Compassion and mindfulness open the door to deep communication — communion. We are no longer separate individuals with different agendas; we enter a place where agendas do not matter. Within communion, we practice intentional discernment to find consensus. Within our communion, which is the deepest level of intuitive response, the stream of our compassionate understanding flows. True understanding, possible only during communion, is the transformative catalyst to any relationship.

Communion is full body listening. St. Benedict in his Rule admonishes us to "listen with the ear of our heart." This, for me, is full body listening. While we listen to the words of another, we are also listening for what is behind the words, for what is not being said, to the body's stance, to the cadence of the words, and nuances of what is being said. We listen with our eyes and pay attention to body language. We engage all of our senses.

"Listening with the ear of our heart" is both an external and internal sensing. In communion we let go of our fears and respond to what our heart hears. We intentionally listen to our internal monologue. We recognize and acknowledge our judgments and assumptions and the roles they play in our ability to communicate. When we are in communion with another, we cannot hide behind our own illusions. We shift from judgment-based reaction to compassion-filled response. In communion we engage our curious daring and courage to stimulate transformation fueled by our compassionate action.

Communion calls us to celebrate our authentic being. We no longer hide behind our assumptions and judgments. We acknowledge and accept our flawed humanity. There is no room for hatred or discouragement. We look with compassion upon our self and unconditionally love those parts we deem unsavory or unwanted. Love provides the impetus for change and deepens not only our relationship with self but with all others.

Through communion, the home of the ultimate compassionate connection, we gain a deep unity with our self, the Sacred, others, and all of creation. With compassion, we share our authentic self with the authentic selves of others. It is through love shared intentionally and unconsciously that we enter communion and finds the joy-filled resident.

Our bridge building begins the moment we are born. We strengthen the base through our foundational awareness. We anchor our four life pillars deeply within this awareness. We grow and sustain the silence in our quiet mind by integrating our commitment to causing no harm, to alleviating suffering, and accepting all of life as it is. Through the Seven Gifts of the Spirit and our

Start Where You Are: Walking in Compassionate Connection 149

contemplative practices, we gain a greater understanding of who we are. We separate what makes us authentic from what is illusion as we practice RI^2.

In the present moment, we live contemplatively. We explore and experiment with formal practices. We discover which ones are better suited for our journey. These practices help us focus our attention on the present moment. These practices are the cables on our bridge. Through our practice, we maintain a tension and a delicate balance of response and reaction. Moment by moment we grow deeper into our contemplative stance. The silence cultivated by these practices flows from our moment of formal practice into our every day life. The deck of our bridge is built with our contemplative spirit. As we cross the bridge, we engage compassion through our intent and action, moment by moment.

RI^2: Reflection, Introspection, & Integration

RI^2 is a contemplative practice that connects our body, mind, spirit, and heart in order to respond compassionately to something in our life.

First, we reflect with our heart. We identify what we feel without making any judgment about those feelings. We observe what is happening in our life and relationships that might relate to what we are feeling.

Second, we introspect using our logical mind. Again, without judgment, we attempt to understand what is truly amiss. We actively search for patterns of reaction.

Third, we integrate our understanding in ways that shift our fear-filled reactions to compassionate responses. More often than not, we change our thinking or behavior because we see that we were thinking and acting out of preconceptions about our self or others, rather than knowledge and understanding. This process, practiced regularly, transforms us. We become more true to our self, and more compassionate of others.

Use the following questions to reflect, introspect, and integrate transformation into your own life. Enter into a reflective place, where you just notice the many potential answers that reside in your quiet mind. Then engage your introspection. How do these responses fit with the reality of who you are? Which ones are authentic and which ones challenge your illusions? Next, integrate what you have learned by embracing what is real and true and letting go of the unreal and the untruthful. Let go of the illusion.

Sit quietly. In the past chapters, you looked at specific situations and relationships with individuals. These questions focus on how you engage others.

- Who are you? Look with curious daring and share who rests in the deepest, most interior place of your being.
- How are you sharing this vulnerable self? How are you coating yourself with illusion?
- How are you connected to your deepest self? In what ways do you connect yourself to others? (How do you engage in relationship?)
- What is your communication style? Name as many moments as you can when you clearly know you had entered into communion with yourself or another.
- How do you share compassion with yourself?
- Create a montage that represents the elements you expressed.

Afterword

The writing of this book and the journey along my bridge of engaging compassion through intent and action did not happen alone. Compassion is a lived experience that only happens in relationship. I have come to this part of my journey with the support of all my relationships — with the Sacred, with my son, with family members, friends, acquaintances, co-volunteers, and many a stranger. With this telling of my journey, I have reconnected with my self, with others, with all creation, and with the Sacred in surprising and mutually compassionate ways.

Without my connection to the Sacred, I would not have recognized the importance of that first memory so many years ago when I first experienced communion. Recollecting on this experience, I recognize a vein of compassion flowing through me probably since birth, and in the following years, I discovered that compassion is always ready to be engaged in the present moment.

I continue to wake from the slumber of my unknowing and focus on the present moment in the silence of my quiet mind. In this silence, those divine, intuitive nudges continue to wake me to the present moment and remind me of my connection to the Sacred. This connection, my divine spark, is the guiding light of awareness that illuminates the whole of my life. The Sacred reminds me who I am — a bringer of compassion in every moment of every day.

I stand on my bridge, but not without looking over my shoulder a time or two. Some of the memories I glimpse are beautifully compassionate; others are painfully hurt-filled. Self-forgiveness has only been possible through self-compassion. I cross the bridge by continuing to repattern my reactions into responses, living in awareness of the moment, and intuitively responding with compassion. Through this journey, I recognize that the real work has occurred silently within me.

My pen to paper and my fingers to the keyboard, I wrote this book to encourage others to engage compassion through their intent and action. The book reflects a contemplative awareness conceived and birthed with and for others. Family, friends, co-volunteers, and strangers made the journey with me. Those who shared, stretched, or helped sync my vision of compassion include:

Co-volunteers at Compassionate Louisville, my Contemplative Community, my son Merlin, my fellow female orphans and male orphan, my beta readers, my editor Jeanne, G.G., my friends, family members, the staff and customers at the Shelbyville Road Starbucks. Of course, I would be remiss if I did not honor all the intimate strangers who gave me many insights into compassion.

Now my real work begins. And, I hope yours as well. Join me in walking, dancing, plodding, building this bridge. Join me in each moment of finding potential compassion hidden within each reaction and shining brightly in each response. Join me as we engage compassion through intent and action. Let us build that bridge.

Biography

Vanessa Hurst has been aware of her practice as a contemplative for over twenty-one years. She is a member of the Coordinating Circle for the Partnership for a Compassionate Louisville. As a practicing contemplative, she intentionally seeks to share compassion with herself, others, and all of creation. This is the natural rhythm of her life. Vanessa holds a master's degree in Natural Health. In her practice as an intuitive healer and spiritual mentor, Vanessa under- stands that living contemplatively and compassionately is the root to healing. For her, compassion is a lived experience, one she hopes will touch all her relationships but most profoundly her relationship with her son, Merlin. She hopes to inspire many to engage compassion through intent and action.

Contact Vanessa at hurst.vanessa@gmail.com

website: www.intentandaction.com

Resources

I acknowledge those who have inspired me: those who encourage me to experience compassion. Their beliefs and life philosophies have inspired me over my lifetime. Today I stand on a bridge that they also conceived of in different ways. Thanks to those who have encouraged me and many others to embrace compassion. My list is not comprehensive; it is personal.

Bach, Richard. *Jonathan Livingston Seagull.* New York: Macmillian, 1970. Print.
Borysenko, Joan. *A Woman's Journey To God.* New York: Riverhead Publishing, 2001. Print
Cannato, Judy. *Field of Compassion: How the New Cosmology Is Transforming Spiritual Life.* Notre Dame: Sorin Books, 2010. Print
Chittister, OSB, Joan. *Wisdom Distilled from the Daily: Living the Rule of St. Benedict.* San Francisco: HarperSanFrancisco, 1991. Print.
Chödrön, Pema. *Comfortable with Uncertainty: 108 Teachings on Cultivating Fearlessness and Compassion.* Boston: Shambhala Publications, 2010. Print.
---. *Living Beautifully: with Uncertainty and Change.* Boston: Shambhala Publications, 2012. Print.
Church, Dawson. *The Genie in Your Genes: Epigenetic Medicine and the New Biology of Intention.* Fulton, CA: Elite Books, 2007. Print.
Cooper, David A. *God Is A Verb: Kabbalah and the Practice of Mystical Judaism.* New York: Riverhead Books, 1998. Print.

---. *Seeing Through the Eyes of God*. Boulder: Sounds True, 2007. Audio CD.

Dennison, Paul E. *Brain Gym: Simple Activities for Whole Brain Learning*. Ventura: Edu Kinesthetics, 1992. Print

Douglas-Klotz, Neil. *The Sufi Book of Life: 99 Pathways of the Heart for the Modern Dervish*. New York: Penguin, 2005. Print.

Dwyer, Wayne W. *There's A Spiritual Solution To Every Problem*. Fort Mill, SC: Quill House Publishing, 2003. Print.

Fox, Matthew. *A Spirituality Named Compassion And The Healing Of The Global Village, Humpty Dumpty And Us*. Minneapolis: Winston Press, 1979. Print.

Fry, OSB, Ed., Timothy. *The Rule of St. Benedict in English*. Collegeville, MN: The Liturgical Press, 1981. Print.

Hahn, Thich Nhat. *Peace Is Every Step: The Path of Mindfulness in Everyday Life*. New York: Bantam, 1992. Print.

Hawkins, David R. *Power Vs. Force*. Carlsbad: Hay House, 2002. Print.

Kabat-Zinn, Jon. *Wherever You Go, There You Are*. New York: Hyperion, 2005. Print.

Kabat-Zinn, Myla and Kabat-Zinn, Jon. *Everyday Blessings: Inner Work of Mindful Parenting*. New York: Hyperion, 1997. Print.

Leong, Kenneth S. *The Zen Teachings of Jesus*. Chestnut Ridge, NY: The Crossroads Publishing Company, 2001. Print.

Merton, Thomas. *New Seeds of Contemplation*. New York: New Directions Books, 1961. Print.

---. *Raids on the Unspeakable*. New York: New Direction Books, 1966. Print.

---. *Thoughts in Solitude*. New York: Farrar, Strauss, Giroux, 1956. Print.

Myss, Caroline, and Shealy, Norman. *The Science of Medical Intuition: Self-Diagnosis and Healing with Your Body's Energy Systems*. Boulder: Sounds True, 2002. Audio CD.

Oliver, Mary. *Thirst: Poems*. Boston: Beacon Press, 2006. Print.

Schultz, Mona Lisa. *The New Feminine Brain: How Women Can Develop Their Inner Strengths, Genius, and Intuition.* New York: Free Press, 2005. Print.

Silberman, Melvin. PeopleSmart: *Developing Your Interpersonal Intelligence.* San Francisco: Berrett-Koehler, 2000. Print.